THE COMMONWEALTH AND THE NATION

BY THE SAME AUTHOR

India and the Commonwealth 1885-1929 (1965)
The Emergence of the Indian National Congress (1971)

THE COMMONWEALTH
AND THE NATION

S.R. MEHROTRA

VIKAS PUBLISHING HOUSE PVT LTD
New Delhi Bombay Bangalore Calcutta Kanpur

VIKAS PUBLISHING HOUSE PVT LTD
5 Ansari Road, New Delhi 110002
Savoy Chambers, 5 Wallace Street, Bombay 400001
10 First Main Road, Gandhi Nagar, Bangalore 560009
8/1-B Chowringhee Lane, Calcutta 700016
80 Canning Road, Kanpur 208004

COPYRIGHT © S. R. MEHROTRA, 1978

ISBN 0 7069 0673 X

1V02M1402

Printed at Delhi Printers, 21 Daryaganj, New Delhi 110002

PREFACE

The essays included in this volume deal with what has been my main academic preoccupation during the last quarter of a century, namely the Commonwealth and India, or, more precisely, the one in relation to the other. I began in the 1950s as a student of British Imperial history. I am currently engaged in writing a history of the Indian National Congress. But, though I have literally moved from empire to nation, I still subscribe to the view I have long held that the one cannot be studied in isolation from the other.

The transformation of the old British Empire into the modern Commonwealth has been one of the most remarkable events of our age and provides a perennial source of interest to the students of history. The subject has a special significance for the students of modern Indian history. It is, in part, a record of India's emergence as a nation. And even where it is not directly and immediately so, it affords a wider perspective which is essential to the proper understanding of India's recent past. It would, for example, be a mistake to examine the history of India under British rule merely as the outcome of her relationship with Great Britain without taking into account the developments, both past and contemporaneous, in other parts of the Empire, for it would mean ignoring some of the most vital and fruitful factors that have gone into its making. Neither logic nor accident but historical experience has been the mainspring of British Imperial history. Nor can it be denied that the history of the British Empire has a certain unity and rhythm of its own.

If the Commonwealth did not exist, it would be impossible to create it. It has been the result of historical growth. And it has been made as much by nationalism in the distant parts of the

Empire as by British statesmanship. Enthusiasts and heretics, imperialists and nationalists—all have contributed to its shaping. It has been truly a work of 'challenge and response'. If Canadians are proud of the fact that their country has played a major part in the long, peaceful evolution through the nineteenth and twentieth centuries which transformed the British Empire into the British Commonwealth, Indians may take pride in the fact that in the evolution of the modern multi-racial Commonwealth their country has played a significant and often a decisive role. The eight essays contained in the present volume aim at bringing out not only how the recent history of India has to no small extent been influenced by her membership of the British Empire-Commonwealth for more than a hundred and fifty years, but also how on several occasions during this long period India has, both by her exertions and by her example, given a tremendous new impetus to the grand conception of the Commonwealth.

I should like to thank the following for permission to make use of the material which was first published by them as articles:
George Allen and Unwin ('The Politics behind the Montagu Declaration of 1917' in C.H. Philips (ed.), *Politics and Society in India*, 1963);
Indian Council of World Affairs ('Gandhi and the British Commonwealth', *India Quarterly*, January-March 1961);
Leicester University Press ('Imperial Federation and India, 1868-1917', *Journal of Commonwealth Political Studies*, November 1961; 'On the Use of the Term "Commonwealth" ', *Journal of Commonwealth Political Studies*, November 1963) ;
Vikas Publishing House ('Nehru and the Commonwealth' in B.R. Nanda (ed.), *Indian Foreign Policy: The Nehru Years*, 1975; 'Mid-Victorian Anti-Imperialists and India', *Indian Economic and Social History Review*, April-June 1976).

Indian Institute of Advanced Study S. R. MEHROTRA
Rashtrapati Nivas, Simla
June 1977

CONTENTS

1	ON THE USE OF THE TERM 'COMMONWEALTH'	1
2	TWO BRITISH EMPIRES?	18
3	MID-VICTORIAN ANTI-IMPERIALISTS AND INDIA	33
4	IMPERIAL FEDERATION AND INDIA, 1868-1917	49
5	INDIA'S REPRESENTATION AT THE IMPERIAL CONFERENCE	62
6	THE MONTAGU DECLARATION OF 1917	75
7	GANDHI AND THE BRITISH COMMONWEALTH	97
8	NEHRU AND THE COMMONWEALTH	110
	Biographical Notes	129
	Notes	135
	Index	163

1

ON THE USE OF THE TERM 'COMMONWEALTH'

Of the many curious things about our Commonwealth nothing is more curious than its name. We have many histories of the Commonwealth. What we need is a history of the word 'Commonwealth' itself. This essay is not the result of any systematic research but is presented in the hope of correcting a few current misconceptions and of inducing some really competent scholar to undertake the task in a more serious and systematic manner.

The term 'Commonwealth' has been well known to English literature ever since the fifteenth century. The *Oxford English Dictionary* gives the first reference to it in *circa* 1470. It is a compound of two words: Common and Wealth. In fact it was at one time usually pronounced as two words, and this pronunciation still occurs occasionally. It was formerly used in five main senses:

1. Public welfare; general good or advantage; common weal.
circa 1470, John Hardyng, *The Chronicle* (ed. H. Ellis, London, 1812), ch. cxxiv, p. 242:
'For cause he dyd the common wealthe sustene.'
1679, Gilbert Burnet, *The History of the Reformation of the Church of England* (London, 1679), p. 17:
'... the Common-Wealth of the whole Realm was chiefly to be lookt at ....'

2. The whole body of people constituting a nation or state, the body politic; a state, an independent community, especially viewed as a body in which the whole people have a voice or an interest.

1509, Edmund Dudley, *The Tree of Commonwealth* (ed. D.M. Brodie, London, 1948), p. 31:
'The common wealth of this realme ... may be resemblid to a faier and mighte tree ....'
1690, John Locke, *The Second Treatise of Civil Government* (ed. J. W. Gough, Oxford, 1946), p. 165:
'By commonwealth, I must be understood all along to mean, not a democracy, or any form of government, but any independent community which the Latins signified by the word *civitas* ....'
1778, David Williams, *Unanimity in All Parts of the British Commonwealth, Necessary to Its Preservation, Interest and Happiness* (London, 1778), p. 25:
'The British commonwealth (for I will still include America in that idea) is divided into several parts, which may be considered as the several branches of the same family.'
1907, David Lloyd George, *Minutes of Proceedings of the Colonial Conference*, 1907, Cd. 3523, p. 362:
'The federation of free Commonwealths is worth making some sacrifice for.'

3. A state in which the supreme power is vested in the people; a republic or democratic state.
1766, Oliver Goldsmith, *The Vicar of Wakefield*, ch. xx, *Works* (London, 1854), vol. i, p. 399:
'... I found that monarchy was the best government for the people to live in, and commonwealths for the rich.'
1867, James Bryce, 'The Historical Aspect of Democracy', *Essays on Reform* (London, 1867), ch. x, p. 277:
'Government by a class is always government for a class; a Commonwealth therefore knows nothing of classes ....'

4. Specifically, (*a*) English history: the republican government established in England between the execution of Charles I in 1649 and the Restoration in 1660; (*b*) United States history: the official designation of Massachusetts, Pennsylvania, Virginia, and Kentucky; (*c*) Australian history: the federation of Australia since 1901.

5. Figuratively: a body or a number of persons united by some common interest as, e.g., the commonwealth of learning, of mankind, or of Christendom.

1790-91, James Wilson, *Lectures on Law, Delivered in the College of Philadelphia, in the Years 1790 and 1791, Works* (Philadelphia, *1804*), vol. i, p. 45:
'I will view man as an individual, as a member of society, as a member of a confederation, and as a part of the great commonwealth of nations.'
1886, *Fifty Years Progress, the Special Number of Imperial Federation*, the Journal of the Imperial Federation League, June 1886, Introductory, p. iii:
'Sir John Harrington, as Mr. Froude tells us, built his castle in the air some 300 years ago ... and called it "Oceana"—the Great Commonwealth of English-speaking nations, united under one law, by one instinct and purpose, and established throughout the world.'
1887, Bipin Chandra Pal, *The National Congress* (Lahore, 1887), p. 9:
'... I know that without the help and tuition of this Government my people shall never be able to rise to their legitimate place in the commonwealth of civilised nations ....'
1906, Arthur Sawtell, 'India under British Rule', *Proceedings of the Royal Colonial Institute*, 1905-6, vol. xxxvii, p. 290; 'India is not a part of that commonwealth of nations which the United Kingdom and the Britains beyond the seas compose.'

The most common use of the term 'Commonwealth' was in sense 2, and it was in connexion with this that senses 3, 4 and 5 were developed. The term was perhaps more frequently used in the sixteenth, seventeenth and eighteenth centuries than in the nineteenth, when it lost ground to its rivals 'Nation' and 'State'.[1] The establishment of Oliver Cromwell's government in England in 1649 with the title of 'Commonwealth' gave a republican flavour to the term. But, though in the popular mind it acquired anti-monarchical associations[2] and writers like John Dryden, Oliver Goldsmith and Edward Freeman used it in the sense of a republic, the old, established usage of the term in sense 2 persisted. Thomas Hobbes, John Locke and Edmund Burke used the term, as Thomas Smith and William Shakespeare had used it before them, in the sense of a community or state, without reference to the form of government. But the idea of common weal or public good was almost inseparably associated with the term 'Commonwealth'[3] and it was seldom applied to an autocracy. The term easily lent itself to the description of a league, alliance, concert, confederacy, union, or federation, and its use in this connexion, especially to describe the American Union and the Australian Federation, gave it a certain federalist overtone. The figurative use of the term to suggest the idea of a wider political or religious union of mankind made it the vehicle of universalist aims and aspirations.

In a speech delivered at Adelaide on 18 January 1884, which was probably dismissed at the time as a piece of post-prandial oratory but became so famous fifty years later, Lord Rosebery enquired of his Australian audience: 'Does this fact of your being a nation, and I think you feel yourselves to be a nation, imply separation from the Empire? God forbid! There is no need for any nation, however great, leaving the Empire, because the Empire is a commonwealth of nations.'[4] Lord Rosebery might have been the first to describe the British Empire as 'a commonwealth of nations', but he certainly did not coin the phrase. The credit for coining and popularizing the phrase 'commonwealth of nations' should go to the writers on international law.[5] Lord Rosebery was using the phrase, which had been well known for about a hundred years, in a purely descriptive sense. He was not coining a new name for the British Empire. This is conclusively proved by the following extract from his Rectorial address delivered before the students of the University of Glasgow on 16 November 1900: 'I admit the term [Empire] is constantly prostituted in Britain as well as elsewhere. And yet we cannot discard it, for there is no convenient synonym. If any other word can be invented which as adequately expresses a number of states of vast size under a single sovereign I would gladly consider it. But at present there is none. And in the meantime the word Empire represents to us our history, our tradition, our race. It is to us a matter of influence, of peace, of commerce, of civilisation, above all a question of faith.'[6] As far as the present writer knows, Lord Rosebery never again used the phrase 'commonwealth of nations' or 'commonwealth' in connexion with the British Empire. Though he often used the word 'commonwealth', both before and after 1884[7]—it occurs not less than three times in his Rectorial address at Glasgow itself[8]—he invariably used it in sense 2 (a nation or state; the body politic; a community) and not as a synonym for Empire.

Lord Rosebery's description of the British Empire in 1884—even when restricted to its white members—as 'a commonwealth of nations' was far from being accurate. With the colonies in Australia and South Africa still to be federated, there were not many 'nations' in the British Empire in 1884; nor could they be said to form 'a commonwealth'. Moreover, as Professor Mansergh rightly points out,[9] for the notion of a commonwealth of nations the closing decades of the nineteenth century in Britain, with their exuberant and thrustful imperialism, were inhospitable years. All this may probably explain why Lord Rosebery did not use the phrase again and also why it did not 'catch on'. But, however inaccurate or inopportune, Lord Rosebery's remark at Adelaide in January 1884 did indicate his awareness of the fact that the white colonies were fast growing in self-government and national consciousness. A part of the Empire was ceasing to be 'empire'. As applied to the self-governing white colonies, the term 'Empire' was becoming a misnomer. Terminology was beginning to leg behind the facts of the Empire. The so-called anti-imperialists were already busy driving home this point. 'The Imperial relation', wrote Lord Blachford in 1877, 'only subsists in substance between the United Kingdom on the one hand and India and the Crown Colonies on the other. It subsists in form and in form only between the United Kingdom and the constitutional colonies.'[10] 'An empire it is called', remarked Goldwin Smith in 1878, 'but the name is applicable only to India. The relation of England to her free colonies is not in the proper sense of the term imperial . . . .'[11] Seeley admitted in 1883: 'The word Empire seems too military and despotic to suit the relation of a mother-country to colonies.'[12] The white self-governing colonies were no longer 'colonies'. The relationship of the mother country with them was ceasing to be imperial. Clearly, a new term was needed to describe more accurately the changed and changing relationship of Great Britain with her colonies of settlement. In 1900 Bernard Shaw wrote in *Fabianism and the Empire* that 'the words Empire, Imperial, Imperialist, and so forth are pure claptraps, used by the educated people merely to avoid dictionary quibbles, and by the uneducated people in ignorance of their ancient meaning. What the colonies are driving at is a Commonwealth; and that is what the English citizen means, too, by the Empire, when he means anything at all.'[13] In 1905 John Xavier Merriman, the Cape statesman, to whom the words

'Empire' and 'Imperial' had always been 'something of a red rag'[14] and who had ever since the 'eighties been fond of referring to the British Empire as 'the British Commonwealth'[15] actually suggested that the word 'Commonwealth' should be substituted for the word 'Empire' to describe the relationship of Great Britain with the self-governing colonies. Replying to a letter from the British Empire League suggesting that, in order to maintain some sort of continuity in the deliberations of the periodical Colonial Conference, there should be formed something in the nature of an 'Imperial Council', with a permanent committee to examine and report on topics of common interest, Merriman wrote on 1 August 1905: 'Now the word "Empire", which is a perfectly correct one to use as regards the relation of England to India, and to other communities which do not enjoy representative institutions, is clearly not a proper description of the self-governing communities.... The name "Empire", which is generally used to describe the various communities that acknowledge allegiance to the King of England, may serve as a convenient expression for the somewhat undefined relation that has hitherto so happily existed between England and the self-governing communities of English-speaking men; but if this relation is to be made the subject of any sort of written Constitution, I venture to think that "Commonwealth" and not "Empire" more nearly expresses the sort of relation that must exist in the future if the connexion is to be a permanent one.' [16]

The imperialists were not unaware of the rapid development of self-government in the white colonies. In fact it was their uneasiness at this development and their fear that the white colonies might drift into complete independence of the mother country which prompted them to devise schemes of imperial federation. The imperialists, too, were experimenting with new names for their ideal of a united Empire. They called it 'Greater Britain', 'the United States of Britain', 'the British Commonwealth',[17] etc.

Most of the early enthusiasts for imperial federation in the 'seventies and the 'eighties were, however, inclined to believe that the white colonies were a mere expansion of England. This erroneous belief precluded them from fully appreciating the fact that the white colonies were fast developing a national consciousness and a sense of individuality of their own. But the failure of their attempts at closer union of the Empire brought home, at least to the more enlightened imperialists, an increased awareness of colonial nationalism. Joseph Chamberlain described the self-governing colonies as 'sister nations' in 1897.[18] 'Almost imperceptibly', commented a writer in the *Edinburgh Review* of July 1900, 'our forms of speech and our metaphors become modified to suit modern conditions, and our colonial secretary rightly feels, when he referes to the Empire, that it is time to substitute for the old phrase "Mother Country and her Colonies" the more accurate expression of "Sister Nations"—nations, that is, owing a hearty and voluntary allegiance to a common flag, while in all other respects they enjoy the privileges and bear the burdens of independent States.'[19] In 1897 the Canadian preferential tariff had inspired Rudyard Kipling to write:

'A Nation spoke to a Nation,
A Throne sent word to a Throne:
"Daughter am I in my mother's house,
But mistress in my own. . . ." '[20]

In 1900 he welcomed the Commonwealth of Australia 'in the Hall of the Five Free Nations' as 'Daughter no more but Sister'.[21] On 28 October 1901 Alfred Milner told a Durban audience what he meant by 'the great term, the British Empire': 'a group of sister nations spread throughout the world, united and not divided by the ocean, each independent in its own concerns, all indissolubly allied for a common purpose, all free and willing subjects of the most ancient and august Monarchy in the world'.[22] In a speech at Johannesburg on 31 March 1905 he conceded that the words 'Empire' and 'Imperial' were 'in some respects unfortunate' as they suggested 'domination, ascendancy, the rule of a superior state over vassal states'.[23]

Richard Jebb was already busy acquainting the British people with the facts of colonial life. He told them that their popular habit of alluding to the self-governing white colonies as 'the Expansion of England' or 'Greater Britain' was anachronistic, that Canada, Australia and New Zealand were becoming distinct nations, and that their attitude towards the mother country was changing, national patriotism taking the place of colonial loyalty.[24] Joseph Chamberlain remarked on 2 January 1906 that the time had gone by when the white colonies could be spoken of as though they were subject to British dictation. 'They are self-governing nations. They are sister-States,'[25] he added. 'In the economy of the Imperial household', Lord Curzon remarked in December 1907, 'we are dealing not with children but with grown men. At our table are seated not dependants or menials but partners as free as ourselves, and with aspirations not less ample or keen.'[26] On the eve of the Colonial Conference of 1907 Lord Milner wrote: 'True it is, and we ought to rejoice at the fact that the great Colonies have attained, or are fast attaining, as nations, a growing sense of individuality, a character, a pride, and a tradition of their own.'[27] But nationhood, in his view, did not necessarily involve a wholly separate and self-contained existence. 'There may be, there are, cases in which several nations form a single State, or a State-group, possessing political unity.'[28] He, however, expressed his dissatisfaction with the word 'Empire'. 'It is indeed difficult', he said, 'to classify what for want of a better term we call the British Empire. It fits into no recognised category, and cannot be accurately described by means of our existing political vocabulary. We are face to face with a new situation, with a relationship of communities which has no precedent in history. To make it a success we require novel institutions. Even to give an adequate account of it we almost require a new terminology. Whoever attempts to describe it is perforce driven to the use of analogy and metaphor. The phrase "a family of States", though lacking in precision, is perhaps best calculated to convey a conception corresponding to the facts.'[29]

Writing in the *Standard of Empire* of 23 May 1908 Lord Milner said that, while the word 'Empire' fairly described the position as between the United Kingdom and subject countries such as India or the Central African possessions, for the relations existing between the United Kingdom and the self-governing colonies it was 'a misnomer, and with the idea of ascendancy, of domination, inevitably associated with it, a very unfortunate misnomer'.[30] It had, he added, the harmful effect of encouraging misunderstandings in the self-governing colonies and false and antiquated notions of imperial unity at home. In an address to the Royal Colonial Institute on 16 June 1908, Lord Milner returned to the theme. 'I often wish', he remarked, 'that when speaking of the British Empire . . . we could have two generally recognised appellations by which to distinguish the widely different and indeed contrasted types of states of which that Empire is composed. Contrasted, I mean, from the point of view of their political constitution, though the contrast, no doubt, as a general rule, has its foundation in the racial, or, what comes to the same thing, climatic conditions. I am thinking of the contrast between the self-governing communities of European blood, such as the United Kingdom, Canada, Australia and New Zealand, and the communities of coloured race, Asiatic, African, West Indian, or Melanesian, which, though often enjoying some measure of autonomy, are in the main subject to the Government of the United Kingdom.'[31] He considered the term 'Empire' when applied to the first great division to be 'a misnomer, and a rather mischievous misnomer'.[32] For want of 'convenient sub-titles for the two groups', which he thought was 'certainly very unlucky', Lord Milner himself chose to call one 'the self-governing Empire' and the other 'the dependent Empire'.[33] W.M. Childs wrote in the *National Review* of October 1908: 'It is plain today that the Imperial cause would not be served by representing the Empire as an enlarged edition of English nationality.... It becomes necessary to revise altogether an outworn nomenclature. The terms that belong to history and to sentiment no longer express the current facts.'[34]

The word 'Empire' was not only a misnomer when applied to the self-governing white colonies, it also hurt the growing self-respect and national pride of their inhabitants. The latter did not like to be called 'colonials' as the name had implications of servitude, inferiority and subordination. They were eager to assert their equality with the citizens of the mother country and to separate themselves from the subjects in the dependencies. J.A. Froude had warned in 1886: 'An "empire" of Oceana there cannot be. The English race do not like to be parts of an empire. But a "commonwealth" of Oceana held together by common blood, common interest, and a common pride in the great position which unity can secure—such a commonwealth as this may grow of itself if politicians can be induced to leave it alone.'[35] 'The word "Imperial"', wrote M.H. Hervey, who had spent twelve years in Australia, in 1891, 'has an ill sound in Colonial ears.'[36] And he strongly urged 'the substitution of the word "Britannic"'. In 1900 Arnold White referred to the derogatory implications of the words 'Colony' and 'Colonist' and remarked that 'the word "Colony" is inapplicable to the daughter States of Britain, and the word "Colonist" is unfitted to describe their inhabitants'.[87] 'If it be possible', he said, 'to discover the missing word that shall describe the Queen's white subjects in all parts of the world, a sentimental gain will be recorded.'[38] J.S. Ewart, a Canadian, remarked in 1904: 'We are a colony... but we do not like the word. We feel it carries with it a flavour of inferiority.'[39] And he demanded that the word 'Kingdom' should be substituted for the word 'Colony' or 'Dominion'. A New Zealander wrote to Lionel Curtis in 1911: 'What could be worse to start with than the term "British Empire" to cover five autonomous nations, two of which derive a large part of their population from non-British stock. Do what you will with the word "Empire" you will not rid it of an ungrateful harshness—a persuasion of military and political superiority (cf. an excellent description in the *National Review* of March 1909, by F.S. Oliver, of a British patriot gulping down the word "Imperialism" and pretending that the taste was not unpleasant). "Empire" connotes dependency and is as unsuitable or more so than the word "Colony". It suggests a central control in London on the one hand, and a body of submissive New Zealanders on the other. In short, it is Downing Street over again, and as such it will never be anything but unpleasant to our minds.'[40] He recommended the adoption of the term 'Britannic Realms' in place of the term 'British Empire'.[41] In deference to colonial sentiments the word 'colony' as a description of the self-governing communities beyond the seas had already been officially dropped in 1907. The white colonies had become 'Dominions' and the Colonial Conference had been renamed the 'Imperial Conference'. But Ellis T. Powell told a meeting at the Royal Colonial Institute on 13 June 1911 that 'many Colonial friends have suggested that "United Nations Conference" would be a much better term than "Imperial Conference", because it strikes just the note of nationhood vital to our existence as united nations scattered all over the world, and excluded the idea of a central despotism absolutely foreign to our thoughts'.[42] The colonies were becoming nations. They no longer thought of the British Empire as 'a cluster of subordinate units grouped in deferential pose round an Imperial centre'.[43] 'The British Empire ... [is] a galaxy of independent nations',[44] remarked the Canadian prime minister, Sir Wilfrid Laurier, in 1902. 'We are now a family of nations',[45] declared the

Australian prime minister, Andrew Fisher, in 1911.

There were a few liberals and radicals in England—nicknamed the 'Little Englanders'—who had never liked the words 'Empire', 'Imperial', and 'Imperialism'. To them these words smacked of spread-eaglism, braggadocio, continental or oriental despotism, militarism, violence, territorial aggrandizement, racial domination, and an ever-present menace to freedom at home and peace abroad. They were men who had objected to the assumption of the title of Empress of India by Queen Victoria, assailed the imperial policies of Disraeli and Joseph Chamberlain, opposed every fresh annexation in Asia and Africa, criticized the schemes of imperial federation, and welcomed the progress of self-government in the white colonies. They drew their inspiration not from the Roman Empire but from the Greek Commonwealth. Their ideal of the British Empire was one of equal liberty for the parts and free association of the whole, for the promotion of human welfare. They needed a new term to express their ideal. In 1900 Sir Henry Campbell-Bannerman, who represented all that was best in the 'Little Englander' school of thought, indicated his preference for 'the homely native phrase the British Commonwealth'. Speaking at a dinner in honour of the visiting Australian Federation delegates at the National Liberal Club on 2 May 1900, Campbell-Bannerman was reported by *The Times* to have remarked: 'The proverb ran that there was no rose without a thorn, and there was one thorn in the rose offered by their honoured guests. It lay in the title of "Australian Commonwealth". Where could they find a word more exactly indicating the intent and purpose of that great aggregated community of which we were all proud to be citizens, and which included all the dominions of her Majesty? In that great creation of the energy of our people in the past and in the present we sought only the welfare and prosperity of all and to make the common weal shared by all for the use of all. That was the ideal of our Australian friends, and how could it be better expressed than by the homely native phrase the British Commonwealth? But we had been too late. These enterprising kinsmen of ours from the other end of the world had appropriated the word, and he confessed he owed them a grudge for it.'[4]

When Campbell-Bannerman made this remark the South African War was still going on. That war turned the tide of imperialism which had been flowing unchecked in Britain for over two decades. It discredited the words 'Empire' and 'Imperialism' by associating them with the 'methods of barbarism'[47] and of finance capitalism.[48] It widened the rift between the imperialists and the anti-imperialists in Britain and for the first time placed the former on the defensive. The division between the 'pro-Boers' and the 'anti-Boers' was not simply on the war, it was 'a sincere, fundamental, and incurable antagonism of principle with regard to the Empire'.[49] It was neatly summed up in the title of a book written by Goldwin Smith in 1902, *Commonwealth or Empire*. It had long been the claim of the British imperialists that the British Empire was unique, that it was unlike other empires, both past and present, that it had nothing to do with Caesarism and Bonapartism, that it was not antagonistic to democracy and civil liberty, that, in short, it was not really an empire at all.[50] Faced with the mounting criticism of their opponents, a section of the British imperialists resorted to this old, familiar line of argument in self-defence. We are not, wrote Bernard Shaw in 1900, 'a genuinely old-fashioned Empire, autocratically, oligarchically, bureaucratically governed', 'we are constituted as a democratic Commonwealth'.[51] 'The conception of the British Empire', wrote Henry Newbolt in the same year, 'is that of a commonwealth of States under the hegemony of the oldest and the most powerful of them, each State having a larger or smaller share of autonomy in proportion to its aspirations or its fitness, and those which exhibit no such aspirations or fitness being governed under their own laws by Imperial officers, either directly or through their own chiefs, for the benefit of the particular people and not for the enrichment of the paramount State. It is the highest expression yet reached of the autonomous principle of government. Such military despotisms as the two French Empires are its exact antithesis. They are the last expressions of the autocratic centralising ideal. The fact that the heads of such military despotisms call themselves emperors does not make the States they govern empires in any sense of the word, and least of all in the sense in which the British Commonwealth is an empire.'[52]

The word 'Empire' had fallen on evil days. Its champions in Britain had lost their earlier self-confidence, and they were worsted in the election of 1905-6. The Liberal revival and the rise of Labour emboldened its critics and increased their number. They were joined by the anti-imperialists in the self-governing dominions, in Egypt and India, and in Europe and the United States of America. The imperialists regretfully acknowledged the fact that the word 'Empire' had acquired 'some taint of disagreeable association'.[53] While some of them tried 'to raise it in the scale of language by a new significance',[54] others sought to replace it with a new and better word. J. Stanley Little wrote in 1903: '... assuredly the Commonwealth of English peoples would be a far more appropriate name for a confederacy of England and her colonies, than a title in which the word Empire, or any inflexion thereof, appears.'[55] Henry Newbolt had already since 1900 been popularizing the word 'Commonwealth' through his *Monthly Review*.[56] The word 'Union' was suggested by some,[57] but it came rather late and failed to strike the popular imagination. In 1910 C. Reginald Enock[58] came out with a book entitled *An Imperial Commonwealth*. In 1912 the term 'Commonwealth' was adopted by Lionel Curtis[59] who, along with his friends in the Round Table, did much in later years to publicize it and fill its connotations with new concepts of federalism and liberal imperialism. In 1913 Richard Jebb,[60] and early in 1914 Ben H. Morgan,[61] began using the phrase 'Britannic commonwealth' to express their autonomist conception of imperial unity as opposed to the federalist one advocated by the Round Table.

But, though the term 'Commonwealth', in a variety of forms, had begun to be freely used in connexion with the British Empire long before 1914, it owed its real popularity to the war which broke out in that year. The First World War marked another stage in the decline and fall of the word 'Empire'. The German Empire, by its misdemeanours, brought discredit on all empires. Imperialism became synonymous with Prussianism, with autocracy and militarism, with commercial greed and racial exclusiveness, with the denial of justice and the rights of the smaller nations. In their hour of trial some of the more conscientious British imperialists recalled their own utterances and deeds in the past and were ashamed to realize that they had themselves often been guilty of the sins for which they were now condemning the Germans. 'It comes as rather a shock to us in these days', remarked Philip Kerr in 1915, 'to read some of our imperialist literature in the past and see how perilously near some of us have been to preaching the Prussian brand of Imperialism.'[62] And he went on to add: 'That the spirit of Prussia had brooded over this land is proved by the shortest examination of the history of Ireland.'[63] But while the British Empire shared in the general discredit which the German Empire had brought on all empires, it also shone by contrast with the latter. It was not perhaps altogether chance that one of the very first persons to bring out most clearly and correctly the contrast between the British and German Empires was an Oxford professor of German origin who in 1911 had published a notable book called *The Greek Commonwealth*. In an essay written shortly after the outbreak of the war and entitled 'German Culture and the British Commonwealth',[64] A.E. Zimmern emphasized what he considered to be the distinctive feature of the British Empire. The British Empire embodied, he said, however imperfectly, 'the principle of the Commonwealth', 'Lord Acton's great principle of the State as a living body which lives through the organic union and free activity of its several national members'; it stood for 'the union and collaboration of diverse races and peoples', and it looked forward 'not to the definite establishment, in our day, of the World-State, but only to the definite refutation of the wicked [German] theory of the mutual incompatibility of nations'.[65]

The British imperialists were forced by the war to re-examine their creed and purge it of the Prussian heresy. They had to make pious offerings to the gods of democracy and nationalism in whose names they had gone to war. They had to recognize the separate nationhood of the dominions and even to change their angle of vision with regard to 'the dependent Empire'. The British Empire acquired new meanings and new names during the war. The expressions 'Commonwealth', 'Imperial Commonwealth', 'Britannic Commonwealth', 'Commonwealth of Nations', and 'British Commonwealth of Nations' were on the lips of many men and they meant different things to different men.[66] The imperialists used them as synonyms for the British Empire to distinguish it from the enemy empires and to placate the contemporary distaste for the word 'Empire'; the anti-imperialists to signify their abhorrence of empires and imperialism and their preference for freedom and common weal. The imperial federationists used them to indicate their ideal of the British Empire as an organic union and a super-state; the autonomists to emphasize the need for decentralization and liberty. The nationalists used them to stress their individuality, independence and national status; the internationalists to express their ideal of interstate co-operation and human brotherhood.

The subsequent history of the term 'Commonwealth' is fairly well known and needs no more than a brief recapitulation here in order to bring our own account up to date. The publication early in 1916 of two important books edited by Lionel Curtis, entitled *The Problem of the Commonwealth* and *The Commonwealth of Nations*, gave wide publicity to the term 'Commonwealth' in all parts of the Empire. At the Imperial War Conference in April 1917 Sir Robert Borden referred to the British Empire as 'an Imperial Commonwealth of United Nations'[67] and General Smuts as 'the British Commonwealth'.[68] The Conference passed a resolution putting on record its view that there should be a readjustment of the constitutional relations of the component parts of the Empire after the war and that it should be based upon a full recognition of the dominions as 'autonomous nations of an Imperial Commonwealth, and of India as an important portion of the same'.[69] In a famous speech in London on 15 May 1917 Smuts remarked: 'The British Empire is much more than a State. I think the very expression "Empire" is misleading because it makes people think that we are one community, to which the word "Empire" can appropriately be applied. Germany is an Empire. Rome was an Empire. India is an Empire. But we are a system of nations. We are not a State, but a community of States and nations.'[70] He referred to the crown colonies, protectorates and dependencies included in the Empire and added: '... but beyond them we come to the so-called Dominions, independent in their government, which have been evolved on the principles of your free constitutional system into almost independent States, which all belong to this community of nations, and which I prefer to call "the British Commonwealth of Nations". You can see that no political ideas which have been evolved in the past will apply to this world which is comprised in the British Empire; and any name we have yet found for this group is insufficient. The man who will find a proper name for this system will, I think, do real service to the Empire.'[71] Smuts was not the first man to use the phrase 'British Commonwealth of Nations'. Zimmern had used it in 1914, in his essay 'German Culture and the British Commonwealth',[72] to which reference has already been made and which Smuts had probably read. At the Imperial War Conference in 1918 Smuts repeated the phrase 'British Commonwealth of Nations',[73] while Borden spoke of 'the British Commonwealth',[74] and 'Imperial Commonwealth'.[75] In a confidential memorandum written for the Imperial Conference of 1921 Smuts urged, among other things, the adoption of 'a new name for our group [of the self-governing members of the Empire], such as the British Commonwealth of Nations'.[76] The new name made its first official appearance in Article IV of the Anglo-Irish Treaty of 1921.[77] It was reaffirmed by the Balfour Report[78] in 1926 and by the Statute of Westminster[79] in 1931.

While an attempt was thus made to give a new name to the self-governing territories of the British Empire in order to distinguish them from the non-self-governing territories, there was no clear official pronouncement on the subject of nomenclature and the public were left free to use the expression they liked. The name 'Empire', as Sir Keith Hancock has pointed out,[80] 'proved itself tough' and 'retained the favour of the plain blunt men'. It represented a tradition and a hard political reality in many parts of the world which no amount of prejudice against it could undermine. The term 'Commonwealth', in a variety of forms, was applied indiscriminately by politicians and publicists alike either to the British Empire as a whole or to its privileged inner circle of self-governing members.

As the sun of the British Empire set rapidly after the Second World War, the name 'Empire' went into natural oblivion. The term 'British Commonwealth of Nations', though hallowed by official usage, had never been able to acquire the same currency as the term 'British Commonwealth' or 'Commonwealth', for the simple reason that it was rather too long and could not be adapted for adjectival purposes. The same was true of the term 'Commonwealth of Nations', which, without the qualifying word 'British', had the additional disadvantage of being imprecise and misleading. In recent years the use of both these terms has become rarer. This may probably be due to the fact that the national status of the self-governing members of the Commonwealth today admits of little doubt either in their own eyes or in those of the world, and, therefore, does not need the same emphasis as it did in the 'twenties and the 'thirties. With the addition of many self-govern- Asian and African members to the Commonwealth since 1947 the adjective 'British', too, has fallen into disfavour. The simple, unadorned title 'the Commonwealth' seems to be the most popular today. It is concise and comprehensive. It combines tradition with modernity. It means all things to all men. And though some may regret the passing away of old, familiar landmarks, most people would readily agree with the remark made in 1897 by that famous Australian Commonwealth-man, Sir Edmund Barton: 'Commonwealth is the greatest and most stately name by which a great association of self-governing people can be characterised.'[81]

2

TWO BRITISH EMPIRES?

'*The Two Empires*'

On 31 December 1600 Queen Elizabeth signed the charter of the East India Company. Six years later the Virginia Company was founded. Two enterprises were thus launched at the threshold of the seventeenth century which contained within them the seeds of what have been, rather inappropriately, called 'the British Empire in the East and the British Empire in the West'.[1] For almost three centuries 'East and West pursued their divergent destinies'.[2] It was not until the second decade of the twentieth century that the two began to converge into a unity of purpose which made possible the Commonwealth of today.

When at the Colonial Conference of 1907 the self-governing colonies of the British Empire decided to style themselves 'Dominions'[3] and became, as it were, the peers of the realm, the event underlined an historical fact. The distinction was conferred not merely to emphasize that the white colonies had come of age, but also to indicate—inasmuch as they desired to be marked out from the other parts of the Empire—that their past had been different and their future should be unlike that of their humbler brethren, with a duskier complexion and living in hotter climes.

In an address to the Royal Colonial Institute in London on 16 June 1908 Lord Milner remarked that the British Empire was in fact composed of two groups of states—contrasted from the point of view of their political constitution—the self-governing and the dependent.[4] There were two empires, he said, not one. It was 'very unlucky', he thought, that they had no convenient sub-titles for the two groups—two appellations by which to distinguish the two widely different and contrasted units of which the British

Empire was composed. Their absence, in his view, hampered clarity of thinking and the framing of the right policies about each part, for principles of imperial policy applicable to one were radically false about the other. Milner himself suggested two collective terms for the main divisions into which the British Empire fell— 'the self-governing Empire', including the United Kingdom and the dominions of European blood; and 'the dependent Empire', including India, the crown colonies and the protectorates.[5] The policy which Milner advocated with regard to the former was to be one of union and partnership, with regard to the latter that of retention and profitable development.

The Sphere of Settlement and the Sphere of Rule

What were the factors which had contributed towards the contrasted growth of the two empires? Our main concern here is to find out how the constitutional development of the self-governing colonies came to differ from that of India. According to Milner, it had 'its foundation in racial, or, what comes to the same thing, climatic conditions'.[6] The self-governing colonies were of European extraction and situated in the temperate zones. The dependent empire was peopled by the brown or dark races and lay in the tropics. The explanation, though apparently plausible, is hardly sufficient to satisfy our curiosity. A racial and geographical division of the British Empire corresponded well—broadly speaking—to the facts of the time, but it does not explain the nature of diverse growth. There is need to look deeper.

The self-governing colonies were colonies of settlement. They were 'an Empire of dwelling places' whose keynote was 'reproduction'.[7] They were peopled with a kindred stock, having ties of blood, religion and language with the mother country, who could well be described as Englishmen across the seas. C.W. Dilke coined for them the phrase 'Greater Britain'.[8] True, Canada and South Africa had large populations which had no such affinities, but the French Canadians and the Boers were both Europeans and Christians and thus shared in a larger unity with the British. This was a fact of no small significance in an age when only Europeans were considered to be capable of self-government.

India, on the other hand, was a conquered dependency. Here was a land of old civilizations, with different peoples, strange manners, customs, religions and languages. It belonged to 'the sphere of rule' whose keynote was 'government'.⁹ An alien people and an alien country, with no community of sentiments such as animated the white colonies, occupied a different position in the imperial household from that accorded to the daughter communities.

The colonial soil was favourable to the growth of democracy. The settlers brought representative institutions with themselves as their birthright. On a virgin soil, in a sheltered situation, with an expanding frontier and that 'unusual plasticity'¹⁰ which these favourable circumstances provided to young communities, they established societies freer and more democratic than even the one at home. In the beginning those who stayed at home and those who went out were both the king's subjects and hence equals. Later when Parliament increased its powers and instead of monarchical sovereignty parliamentary sovereignty came to be asserted, the colonials resented the assumption of superiority by the stay-at-homes.¹¹ The Thirteen Colonies rebelled against what they regarded as a usurpation of authority and asserted their own popular sovereignty as opposed to a distant one which they neither made nor controlled. The moral of the loss of the Thirteen Colonies was not immediately learnt, but when it was, it became a prominent factor in the growth of colonial autonomy in the future. A determination to avoid the repetition of 1776 was to be a potent factor in allowing the other colonies to have their way when they appeared to be as unruly and unreasonable as the Thirteen Colonies had been.

The Indian situation was entirely different. Trade led to the acquisition of political rights, and then to annexations and supreme government. The British in India either supplanted or came to terms with indigenous autocrats. Having stepped into the shoes of the Great Mughals, as it were, they naturally aspired and even needed to play the role of their predecessors. In India British rule came nearest to the 'classic-continental' tradition of empire.¹² The Sovereign Company was 'the Company Bahadur' and Queen Victoria took in 1876 the title of 'Kaiser-i-Hind'.¹³ But the British came to India as aliens and stayed as mere sojourners. They were 'in it but not of it'.¹⁴ Settlement on colonial lines was neither possible—mainly because of climatic conditions and the non-availability of land—nor did the East India Company, which was primarily interested in trade, encourage it. Company rule tried to fit into the ruts of the old indigenous order. India was too big and too divided. Indian society was ridden with caste, class and religious differences. Successors to an era of confusion and anarchy, menaced with the ever-present danger of internal disorders and European rivals abroad, the British naturally strove to establish a strong despotic government in India. For a long time neither local traditions nor local needs demanded political concessions. What was wanted was peace, good government and a strong, just and impartial hand. These became the watchwords of the British administration in India.

Administration: Colonial and Indian

In the colonies of settlement representative government was established as a matter of course by emigrant Englishmen who carried with them the traditions more or less firmly established at home.[15] 'The early English colonies', wrote George C. Lewis in 1841, 'were in practice nearly independent of the mother-country, except as to their external commercial relations; and there was scarcely any interference on the part of England with the ordinary management of their internal affairs.'[16] The inheritance of the English common law, the fact of distance, the absence of any system or continuity in imperial policy towards them in the formative stages of their development, and the increasing determination of the colonists to be treated as equals and to have their own way—all made for autonomy and the growth of self-government in the colonies of settlement. Sir Charles Adderley wrote in 1869: '... the acquisition of self-government is not so much the gift of an enlightened policy, as the natural tendency and necessity of English colonies.'[17] The remark, though rather unfair to the mother country, for it fails to recognize her liberality and good sense, has an element of profound truth in it.

The seventeenth century which marked the beginning of British empire-building—mainly as a result of trade and private initiative —was a period of great internal unrest and perpetually changing authority in England; 'there was therefore no continuity or system in colonial administration, and self-government for the colonies grew up in fact if not in name'.[18] By the end of this century 'the centre of gravity of colonial administration had been shifted from England to America'[19] and 'a normal type of organisation, familiar to us as "the old representative system" became established'.[20] The eighteenth century was a time of recurring foreign wars for England, and though a greater continuity in colonial policy was provided, due mainly to the existence of the Board of Trade and Plantations (1696-1782), constant warfare hampered the development of a systematic administration. Troubled times and the growth and maturity of colonial assemblies made for non-interference from home and the refusal of the colonists to accept whatever little there was of control.

When ultimately the state became more prominent in dealing with colonial affairs at the beginning of the nineteenth century, the process of self-government had gone far enough in the colonies of settlement. That the nineteenth century differed materially from the previous ones in British imperial history was due in no small part to scientific inventions, especially steam navigation, the telegraph and the railways. How did these scientific inventions affect the relations between the mother country and the colonies? C.P. Lucas observed: 'It is possible that the facilities for interference supplied by scientific invention, if they had been supplied at an earlier date, might have militated against the grant of responsible government to the present self-governing dominions by removing in a sense the element of distance, which was the main reason for giving responsible government; but by the time that steam and telegraphy had become fully effective, the dominions had reached the stage when self-government was imperative, and could no longer be denied. In regard, therefore, to the relations between the mother country and the self-governing dominions, it may fairly be said that the effect of scientific invention has been distinctly beneficial, as making for a better understanding between the Colonial Office and the dominions, at a stage in history when interference from home, to any substantial extent, had already been discarded, and by multiplying the opportunities for personal visits.'[21]

From the very start the policy and details of the East India Company's operations were strictly regulated by its directors in London. When, prompted by the political situation in India, the Company tended to become a sovereign body, the British Parliament intervened. After a minute and severe parliamentary investigation a dual system was introduced in 1784 which converted the

Company into a quasi-state department.[22] Power in the last resort lay with the Board of Control which supervised political activities and whose president was a member of the British cabinet, but the directors appointed all officials from the governor-general downwards and, backed by a clique in the House of Commons devoted to Indian interests, wielded great influence. Though cumbersome, the dual system worked reasonably well and made possible a systematic, continuous and effective policy in regard to India. The period of conquest and annexation from 1757 to 1858 had needs other than those of political concessions. The task of conquest, consolidation and good administration was all-absorbing. The loss of the Thirteen Colonies had already shifted interest and emphasis from America to India and English statesmen spoke of British India as 'the brightest jewel that now remained in his Majesty's crown'.[23]

The state, which, as noted earlier, came more in evidence in dealing with imperial affairs during the nineteenth century, was marked 'as much in relaxing authority as in asserting itself'.[24] As Lucas wrote: 'It has taken over India from a chartered company, but has conceded self-government in fullest measure to British North America, Australasia, and South Africa.'[25] Steam and telegraph not only contributed to more centralized and effective control in India itself, rapid communication tended to produce stronger and more continuous control over the government of India from England. Whether or not it was more intelligent, it was certainly uniform, consistent and thorough. The secretary of state for India became 'a Great Mogul in a frock coat' and the government of India 'a government by cables'. The influence of of retired Anglo-Indians[26] in Parliament and the India Council was considerable. The authors of the Montagu-Chelmsford Report observed: 'We have no hesitation in saying ... that the interest shown by Parliament in Indian affairs [since 1858] has not been well-sustained or well-informed. ... Indeed, we have the paradox that Parliament ceased to assert control at the very moment when it has acquired it.'[27] And it is difficult to disagree with their conclusion 'that Parliament's omission to institute regular means of reviewing the Indian administration [was] as much responsible as any single cause for our failure, in the face of growing nationalist feeling in India, to think out and work out a policy of continuous advance'.[28]

Mid-Victorian Anti-Imperialism and India

If in the era of what is called mid-Victorian anti-imperialism[29] many in England despaired of retaining the colonies for long and with a wise resignation talked of independence as being their natural destiny, few such thoughts were entertained about India.[30] Even Richard Congreve,[31] John Bright[32] and Goldwin Smith[33] realized that any precipitate withdrawal of British authority from India would mean the return of the old chaos, which would not only be disastrous for India herself but a moral crime on the part of England. A Frenchman wrote at the beginning of the present century: 'The question is not whether England has a right to keep India, but rather whether she has a right to leave it. To abandon India would in truth lead to the most frightful anarchy. Where is the native power which would unite Hindoos and Moslems, Rajputs and Marathas, Sikhs and Bengalis, Parsees and Christians, under one sceptre?'[34] The earlier British forecasts of Indian self-government by men like Munro and Macaulay[35] had either been forgotten or appeared as distant as ever of realization. British trade with India was increasing. More and more British capital was being sunk into the country. The revolt of 1857 had been suppressed, with all its inevitable reaction of racial bitterness, hardening of attitudes and a determination on the part of the British to hold fast to what had been conquered at such a heavy cost. Not a few Englishmen hoped that the Raj would last for ever.[36]

Free Trade and the Empire

The victory of free trade principles in England and the progress of responsible government in the colonies were in a way closely allied not merely because both were the outcome of the same liberal impulses at home, but more so because the repeal of the Corn Laws carried in its train the Enabling Act for separate colonial tariffs and the repeal of the Navigation Acts. The ungrateful colonies, instead of shaping themselves in the image of the imperial mother, resorted to protective tariffs—even against Great Britain—and defied the latter's attempt to tamper with their fiscal autonomy. To political recalcitrance was now added economic recalcitrance and both contributed towards the development of what came to be known as dominion status.

India, however, could be shaped nearer to their hearts' desire by Englishmen. She had no responsible government, which, taking advantage of *laissez-faire* and the Manchester school liberalism in England, could work for greater economic and political autonomy. Indian trade was far more important to England than that of all the colonies put together and the fear that the application of the principles of self-government to India might prove detrimental to the interests of English manufacturers—as colonial experience had shown—made those principles appear all the more suspect to Englishmen.[37]

All these factors, then, and not merely race or climate, go to explain why the constitutional development of India came to differ from that of the white dominions. Contrasted in their origins, their composition, their early history, their needs and circumstances, their courses differed. If 'the British Empire in the East' differed from 'the British Empire in the West', it was due largely to the fact that the metropolitan authority had a different challenge to meet in the one than in the other.

The Rhythm of the British Empire

But was it all such a contrasted growth? Was India so very differently treated by the British? Had the lines of advance in the two empires been so divergent, would it ever have been possible for them to coverage into a unity of purpose like the one witnessed in the Empire-Commonwealth of the twentieth century?

It was not without an element of profound truth that the British Empire was likened to a system of planets moving round a central sun.[38] From the parent body they got their light and warmth. Not only that. The planets influenced each other. It was to such a system that British India belonged. To examine British Indian history in isolation, or merely as the outcome of India's relationship with Britain, without taking into account developments, both past and contemporaneous, in other parts of the British Empire, is to ignore some of the deepest, most essential and most fruitful factors that have gone into its making. As the course of dominion history was decisively influenced by the rise of liberal ideas and feelings in Great Britain, so was the course of Indian history. As the political experience and development of one dominion influenced another, so did they influence India—even if that influence was not always so direct and logical and inevitable. India's political development was determined to a large extent by the fact that she was a part of the British Empire. Even a casual student of British Indian history is likely to be struck by the fact that some of the important landmarks in India's constitutional advance were intimately connected with the progress in one part of the British Empire or another.

Pitt's India Act of 1784—the first Act of Parliament to give the Crown some direct responsibility for the good government of India, 'to give the crown', as Pitt himself said, 'the power of guiding the politics of India with as little means of corrupt influence as possible'[39]—was an offshoot of a reforming movement in Britain which gained its greatest impetus from the feelings aroused by the revolt of the Thirteen Colonies in America. It was also the period which witnessed the rise of the great humanitarian movement which 'awakened British conscience to the fact that the weak and backward peoples of the world, with whom European explorers and traders were now increasingly in contact, could not be excluded by a colour bar from the rights of man or the grace of God'.[40] Evangelicalism not only gave birth to the anti-slavery movement, it also made British imperialism 'self-conscious'.[41] The tales of the misdoings of the servants of the East India Company stirred the consciences of some British statesmen. To Edmund Burke, for example, the power which Britain had acquired in India involved a duty and a responsibility, and he enunciated in this connexion the famous principle 'that all political power which is set over men . . . ought to be some way or other exercised ultimately for their benefit'; its possession and use are, 'in the strictest sense, a trust'.[42]

There was a good deal of arrogance and ignorance implicit in the idea of British trusteeship for India, but the recognition that the British administration in India must conform to British ideals and standards and that power brought with itself a responsibility was to prove momentous in its consequences. The system of government established in India, though different from that prevailing in the white dominions, was still essentially British in its chief characteristics. The ultimate ideals which the more enlightened British administrators set before themselves, the type of civilization they wished to work up to were British no less. And this was a fact of great significance. For though the administrators often tended to mistake good and efficient administration as an end in itself, the mere fact that the source, the manner and the inspiration were essentially British was to prove decisive in the long run, and despite the differences as to time and means the ultimate end to be achieved in India proved to be no different from that in the dominions.

It was fashionable at one time to talk of two different experiments being carried on within the same political complex called the British Empire, each forming a constitutionally separable system: autonomy and partnership in the self-governing part, and retention of profitable control over the dependent empire held in trust for the natives. Time was to prove—as might have been foreseen—that the two experiments aimed at the same results in the long run. An eternal trust was no trust at all. The destinies of the two empires were after all not so divergent as they appeared—or were made out to appear—at one time. The divergence proved to be a matter of pace and methods only. The spirit that inspired the two experiments was the same.

It was in connexion with India that the British for the first time recognized the principle which was more than a century later to be embodied in the Colonial Development and Welfare Act of 1940, namely that imperial policy should not be viewed only as a matter of maintaining law and order, but should aim at an active and systematic promotion of native welfare.[43] The two reasons that the younger Pitt gave for bringing British activities in India under the control of Parliament were to 'confirm and enlarge the advantages derived to this country [Great Britain] from its connexion with India' and 'to render that connexion a blessing to the native Indians'.[44] In 1813, at the renewal of the charter of the Company, Lord Grenville laid down that the welfare of the people of India was one of the triple purposes of British imperial policy.[45] The Charter Act of 1833, which enunciated the important political principle of the equality of all the king's subjects before the law,[46] was no fortuitous event. It was the act of the first reformed Parliament which was the crowning achievement of that reforming and humanitarian movement of which mention has already been made. If the common law provided the colonies of settlement with their shield and anchor, wrote E. Barker, the equity idea and the practice of the trust became the Magna Carta for the colonies by conquest or cession.[47] True, between the idea and the reality a sinister shadow often fell and a mischievous time-lag intervened, and words of promise uttered to the ear were at times broken to the heart, but looking back on the history of British rule in India as a whole, we cannot fail to admit the truth contained in C.P. Lucas's epigrammatic remark that 'British colonial policy may be summed up as an attempt to harmonise what ought to be done with what has been said'.[48] The steady reform of law and administration and the introduction of English education, whose influence on the course of Indian political development was to be far-reaching, were all inspired by that Whig liberalism which transformed the face of English society and state.

In 1861 came the Indian Councils Act. Much had happened in India, Great Britain and the Empire between 1833 and 1861. The revolutionary spirit of Europe had entered British politics. The Chartist movement had left its mark. The realization had dawned on the ruling elite in Britain that political power would have to be extended to the lower classes. Durham had written his famous report and Canada had won responsible government and fiscal autonomy. When after the suppression of the revolt of 1857 the Crown took over the governance of India from the East India Company and overhauled the system of administration, a non-official element was introduced into the central and provincial legislative councils in India. It was undoubtedly a very cautious and partial introduction, but what was important was that it was done. The character of government remained autocratic, but autocracy was being tempered by the introduction of institutions and principles of a very different kind which were one day to prove to be the cause of its undoing.

The progress of autonomous government in the colonies, the enfranchisement of the working classes and the triumph of Gladstonian liberalism in Britain, and the campaign for Irish home rule found their reflex in India. The introduction of local self-government in India by Mayo in 1870-1 and its extension under Ripon in 1883, and the birth of the Indian National Congress in 1885 owed a great deal to the stimulus provided by outside events and forces. Stirrings of political life outside coupled with those in India led to the Indian Councils Act of 1892. Implemented under Cross and Lansdowne, but based on the suggestions originally made by Dufferin—who had been governor-general of Canada before coming out to India in 1884—the Act of 1892 not only strengthened and extended the principle of representation already granted, but also gave the people a voice in choosing their representatives. Dufferin denied that his proposals implied 'an approach ... to English parliamentary government and an English constitutional system',[49] as Ripon had denied that he was 'trying to impose our English system on India'.[50] Disclaimers, however, proved unavailing, for practice outran theory. What was even more significant was the fact that unconsciously, almost instinctively, the 'English system' had been introduced in India. Groping in the dark as they still were, the only 'light of political science and of history' which they had to guide their steps was that of British and imperial history. The letter denied but the spirit gave life.

The Morley-Minto reforms of 1909 were the work of the great Liberal ministry which extended responsible self-government to the erstwhile Boer republics of the Transvaal and the Orange Free State and made possible the Union of South Africa. The vastness and the diversity of India still made it impossible for most Englishmen to envisage a self-governing India on democratic lines. Both Morley and Minto emphatically denied that their reforms were aimed at the establishment of a parliamentary government in India.[51] But Morley put his finger on a profound truth, which had been and was to continue to be the motive force of British policy in India, when he wrote to Minto in 1906: 'Not one whit more than you do I think it desirable or possible, or even conceivable, to adapt English political institutions to the nations who inhabit India. Assuredly not in your day or mine. But the *spirit* of English institutions is a different thing, and it is a thing that we cannot escape even if we wished, which I hope we don't. I say we cannot escape it, because British constituencies are the masters, and they will assuredly insist—all parties alike—on the spirit of their own political system being applied to India.'[52]

Whatever the views of individual governors-general and secretaries of state, however limited their objective or gaze, what counted in the long run was the slow but steady operation of those principles of political progress which had guided the destinies of Britain and her Empire elsewhere—almost as if they were the laws of British imperial development. Parliament might seem to be 'a sleepy guardian', the British public might appear to be indifferent and unconcerned, and attempts might occasionally be made to restrict the application of British ideas to India, but their influence in determining the fortunes of India proved to be the most decisive.

The Duke of Wellington is said to have remarked that, 'If ever we lose India, it will be Parliament that will lose it for us'.⁵³ To Minto the House of Commons was 'perhaps the greatest danger to the continuance of our rule in this country'.⁵⁴ Morley, however, was never tried of reminding the viceroy and the British officials in India that they were 'servants and agents of a Parliament in a free country'⁵⁵ and that 'the British demos [had] its queer eye upon them'.⁵⁶ 'Does it strike you as odd', he asked Minto, 'that, in spite of elephants, salaams, and God Save the King fifty times a day, all depends on that rather inscrutable being, the elector of the United Kingdom?'⁵⁷ As to British ideas, it had long since been foreseen that the imperial eagle would one day be transfixed by the dart which was feathered with its own wing. 'Many', said Winston Churchill in the House of Commons in the India debate of 1947, 'have defended Britain against her foes. None can defend her against herself.'⁵⁸ In these words we have a commentary on British rule in India and on the British policy of liberal imperialism in general.

The Dominion Model

By the first decade of the twentieth century the dominions had reached a definite stage in their political development. Having gained autonomy in internal self-government and fiscal matters they were ready to reach out for it in external affairs. Indian nationalists had hitched their wagon to the dominion star and put forward a claim for self-government for India on the dominion model. At first it was considered to be impracticable, even inconceivable, by most British statesmen.⁵⁹ Morley told the Indian nationalist leader G.K. Gokhale that it was 'a mere dream'.⁶⁰ But Gokhale was not discouraged, for he knew that 'the genius of the British people, as revealed in history, on the whole made for political freedom, for constitutional liberty',⁶¹ and that 'there was room in the Empire for a self-respecting India' as 'the cases of the French in Canada and the Boers in South Africa showed'.⁶² Moreover, had the British government any alternative as long as it remained British and pursued the policy of 'Order *plus* Progress'?⁶³ Could it for ever refuse to recognize the goal of self-government on the dominion model for India as valid? As the Montagu-Chelmsford Report put it in 1918: '. . . step by step British policy in India has been steadily directed to a point at which the question of a self-governing India was bound to arise . . . .'[64] And it went on to say: 'The demand that now meets us from the educated classes of India is no more than the right and natural outcome of the work of a hundred years. Unless we are right in going forward now the whole of our past policy in India has been a mistake.'[65]

The British Commonwealth of Nations

The First World War increasingly brought home to many people in Great Britain the realization that it was not enough to maintain order and give good government to a subject people, the latter must gradually be enabled to do these jobs themselves. The war reinforced the assault of democracy and nationalism on the imperial idea and led to an anxious re-assessing of imperial values. The very words *Empire* and *Imperialism* became suspect and fell into disfavour as savouring of power and domination, militarism and racial pride. Many in England felt that the spirit of Prussia had brooded over their own island and that some of their own countrymen had preached the Prussian heresy in the past.[66] When, therefore, the question of the goal of British rule in India was raised during the war, there seemed to be only one response, consistent with logic and history, tradition and faith, and it was the one that E.S. Montagu, the secretary of state for India, made in the House of Commons on 20 August 1917. 'The policy of His Majesty's Government,' he declared, 'with which the Government of India are in complete accord, is that of the increasing association of Indians in every branch of the administration, and the gradual development of self-governing institutions, with a view to the progressive realisation of responsible government in India as an integral part of the British Empire.'[67]

With the declaration of 20 August 1917 the destinies of the two British empires converged. Taken together with the admission of India to the Imperial Conference four months earlier, it signified the passing away of the Second British Empire and the beginning of what A. E. Zimmern called 'the Third British Empire',[68] the transformation, in principle, of the Empire into a Commonwealth of Nations. On 16 February 1788 Edmund Burke had protested against what he called 'a plan of geographical morality, by which the duties of men, in public and in private situations, are not to be governed by the relation to the great Governour of the Universe, or by their relation to mankind, but by climate, degrees of longitude, parallels not of life but of latitudes'.[69] The Montagu announcement did away with the 'geographical morality' of British imperial policy. That announcement, says Zimmern, 'is a landmark in British imperial history. It marks the definite repudiation of the idea that there can be, under the British flag, one form of constitutional evolution for the West and another for the East, or one for the white races and another for the non-white.'[70]

3

MID-VICTORIAN ANTI-IMPERIALISTS AND INDIA

Towards the close of his pioneering and painstaking *Studies in Mid-Victorian Imperialism*, C. A. Bodelsen remarks: 'It will have been observed that the questions connected with British rule in India (and still more those connected with the Crown Colonies) attracted comparatively little attention from the Imperialists of the seventies and eighties, who were mainly concerned about the possibility of a closer union between England and what would now be called the Dominions, just as the Separatists had mainly concentrated on the latter, because [the] self-governing colonies offered an easier target for their arguments than the possessions proper.'[1] This article is intended to be a commentary, with particular reference to India, on the latter half of Bodelsen's remark.

Let us begin by recapitulating the main arguments of the so-called separatists or anti-imperialists of the mid-Victorian period. The fundamental proposition from which most separatists, both 'active' and 'passive', started was the supposed lesson of the loss of the Thirteen Colonies under painful and humiliating circumstances and the emancipation of large parts of the Spanish and Portuguese empires, for they justified, in their opinion, the truth of Turgot's remark, that colonies were like fruits, which cling to the tree only till they are ripe. The contemporary current of British colonial history—'the perpetual assertion of the right to self-government'[2]—pointed to the same moral. The very success of the experiment in responsible government in the British colonies, because it led to the gradual crumbling away of the remnants of imperial control, weakened the faith in the retention of the colonies, or even in its desirability. 'These wretched colonies', wrote Benjamin Disraeli to Lord Malmesbury in 1852, 'will all be independent in a few years, and are a millstone round our necks.'[3] In 1866 he was asking: 'What is the use of these colonial dead-weights *which we do not govern?*'[4] To Richard Cobden it was 'ironical' to talk of the loyalty of the 'people who neither pay our taxes nor obey our laws, nor hold themselves liable to fight our battles, who would repudiate our right to the sovereignty over an acre of their territory, and who claim the right of imposing their own customs duties, even to the exclusion of our manufactures'.[5]

The separatists asked: if the colonies were bound to cut the cable sooner or later, why should the mother country go on incurring large sacrifices for their sake, more so when these sacrifices brought no sufficient *quid pro quo* even in the present? Why should the mother country spend about £3,000,000 annually on imperial troops in the colonies while the latter misappropriated the waste lands, refused to take convicts and excluded British goods? Clearly, the tie was 'one-sided'. Economy was the watchword of the day, and the colonies were expensive. It was fashionable to draw up a balance-sheet of the advantages and disadvantages accruing from the possession of the colonies and to show that the latter outweighed the former. The advantages were non-existent or would continue to exist even after the colonies became independent, assured the separatists. The moral was self-evident: prudence demanded that the mother country should prepare the burdensome colonies for independence rather than wait for partings in anger.

Another reason advanced for getting rid of the colonies as early as possible was that their possession brought with it an increased danger of war. The anxieties of guarding the Canadian frontier at the time and the 'native wars' in New Zealand and South Africa were both costly and onerous. The pacifism and antimilitarism of the Manchester School were opposed to incurring increased military liabilities and risks. And not even the staunchest protagonist of the colonial connexion hoped at that time that the colonies would come to the aid of the mother country in her wars outside their frontiers.

England's trade with the colonies in the mid-Victorian period was a mere peddling affair compared with the stupendous exchange she had developed with the rest of the world. That trade did not follow the flag appeared to have been conclusively proved by the fact that the new United States of America was a better customer by far than even the Thirteen Colonies had been. With most Englishmen at the time free trade was not only a sound economic policy but a great moral dogma. When, therefore, the colonies refused to follow the wise and virtuous lead given by the mother country and instead began to levy protective duties, not only on foreign but also on English goods, it was thought that the 'insolent and disobedient' children had committed a heinous moral offence and should be repudiated by the parent.

The attitude of at least some separatists towards colonial independence was not of 'good riddance' but of 'good luck'. They contemplated the 'inevitable day' not with 'resigned expectation' but with enthusiasm. Considering empire and liberty to be irreconcilable, they declared themselves for liberty. Colonial status meant subjection, the retardation of the political growth and material prosperity of the colonies. Independence would develop their sense of nationality and economic well-being as it had done in the case of the Thirteen Colonies.

Most of the considerations which weighed with the separatists in regard to the self-governing colonies did not apply to India. India was, and was generally so regarded by contemporary British politicians and publicists as, a case *sui generis*. 'India', wrote Goldwin Smith, 'stands on a footing of its own, apart from the other dependencies of our Empire.'[6] The loss of the Thirteen Colonies which played such a prominent part in determining the psychology of the separatists was compensated in part by the establishment of British dominion in India. If the Thirteen Colonies had like a ripe fruit fallen from the tree, India like a ripe fruit had fallen into the lap of the East India Company. The pain, the humiliation, and the loss of territory suffered by the British on the American continent had been retrieved to a large extent by calling a new empire into existence in Asia in order to redress the balance of the old. Clearly, 'the brightest jewel that now remained in his Majesty's crown'[7] was to be preserved. The re-conquest of India after the revolt of 1857 served only to strengthen this determination.

'A self-governing dependency', G. Cornewall Lewis had written in 1841, 'is a contradiction in terms.'[8] India was no self-governing dependency and the Indian empire no contradiction in terms. 'The self-governing colonies are not an empire at all', wrote Goldwin Smith, but the 'British Empire in India is empire in the true sense of the term, since Hindustan is governed with imperial sway'.[9] Britain did govern India and India paid 'British' taxes, obeyed 'British' laws, and fought 'Britain's' battles. She added not only to the prestige, but also to the power of Great Britain. While the colonies steadily encroached on the imperial domain and appeared to be preparing to cut the painter, more and more of India was being painted red. How contrasted did the manifest destiny of the British Empire appear in the first half of the 19th century in the two spheres. While the inevitability of disruption of the colonial empire haunted many reflecting Britons, Fate seemed to have willed otherwise in India, where the Company's dominions went on extending, often in spite of its wishes to the contrary.

While the mother country incurred huge sacrifices for the sake of the colonies, India was self-supporting in administration and defence. India paid for her own conquest and she continued to pay handsomely for being ruled by the British. Unlike the colonies, she paid for 'her army' and 'her wars'. James Mill, the peace-loving philosophical radical, who considered the colonies to be a fruitful source of wars and of little use to their possessor, was as anxious as the militant pro-consul Lord Wellesley that 'every inch of ground within the limits of India were subject to [British] sway'.[10] Cobden noted with regret in 1853: 'Public opinion in this country has not hitherto been opposed to any extension of our dominion in the East. On the contrary, it is believed to be profitable to the nation, and all classes are ready to hail with approbation every fresh acquisition of territory, and to reward those who bring us home title-deeds, no matter, I fear, how obtained, to new Colonial possessions. So long as they are believed to be profitable, this spirit will prevail.'[11]

India probably purchased more of British goods at this time than all the self-governing colonies put together. Nor did she practise—in fact, she was not allowed to practise—the protectionist heresy. It was easy for the separatists to argue with an air of plausibility that Britain's trade with the colonies would not suffer even if they became independent. But the same could not be said of India. As Charles W. Dilke pointed out: 'Were we to leave Australia or the

Cape, we should continue to be the chief customers of those countries: were we to leave India or Ceylon, they would have no customers at all; for falling into anarchy, they would cease at once to export their goods to us and to consume our manufactures.'[12] The flag followed the trade in India, but if the trade was to be maintained the flag must continue flying!

Nor could it be argued in the case of India that the British connexion was retarding her intellectual, political and material growth. 'The principle of Colonial Emancipation does not apply to India,' said Goldwin Smith, 'because it is a conquered country, not a Colony; and to throw up the government without making any provision for the preservation of order when we are gone, would be to do a great wrong to the people in addition to those which we have already done.'[13] There were few qualms of conscience on the part of the British with regard to their possession of India, because they considered it necessary for her own civilization. Exeter Hall and Manchester represented the two most powerful groups interested in India in the mid-Victorian period. The one wanted to civilize India by making her accept Christianity, the other by making her grow more cotton. But both were agreed that India should continue to be ruled by the British for a long, long time to come.

But, however unique, India was a part—probably the most important part—of the British Empire. No significant trend of imperial thinking in Britain could, therefore, fail to take her into account or to affect her. India did not offer an easy target for the arguments of the mid-Victorian separatists, but she did not entirely escape their attention either. This point can be easily proved by referring to the writings and speeches of Richard Cobden, John Bright, Richard Congreve, and Charles W. Dilke.

Cobden believed that England had undertaken a perilous and hopeless task in governing India. God and nature had opposed visible and insuperable obstacles to the success of such a rash and audacious scheme.[14] He always watched the affairs in India with a jealous and critical eye and condemned 'the deeds of violence and injustice which have marked every step of our progress in India'.[15] The Indian government was a military despotism and the seat of unsafe finance.[16] He saw no advantage in the possession of India either to the rulers or to the ruled.[17] England had been constantly violating the moral law in that country; she could not continue doing so for all time with impunity.[18] 'And if it be true,' he wrote to Bright in 1857, 'as even Voltaire believed it to be, that there is *"un Dieu retributeur et vengeur"*, the deeds perpetrated by the British in times past, and still more the bloody deeds now being enacted, and which all arise from our original aggression upon distant and unoffending communities, will be visited with unerring justice upon us or our children.'[19] He could see no point in England's possession of India. It was unconnected with free trade and put a challenge to British virtue that could never be met, for no men were that virtuous.[20] He had said all this in 1853 when the Company's charter was under discussion and in his pamphlet, *How Wars Are Got Up in India*. The revolt of 1857 confirmed him in his gloomy and rare wisdom. He despaired of reforming Indians, who 'after a century of intercourse with us... suddenly exhibit themselves greater savages than any of the North American Indians'.[21] He despaired also of his own countrymen in India who were 'descending to a level with these monsters'.[22] He saw increased difficulties in the future, for he feared that the revolt had placed an impassable gulf between the two peoples and that India might become a financial and military liability to England.[23] He wished the Company abolished, because it was a screen between the English nation and a full sight of its awful responsibilities in India, but he doubted the wisdom and the feasibility of the Crown governing India under the control of Parliament. Not only was it impracticable, it might even impair English liberty and character.[24] 'How are we to maintain despotic sway in future over 1,000,000,000 of Asiatics and preserve our freedom at home?'[25] 'Is it possible that we can play the part of despot and butcher there without finding our character deteriorated at home?'[26] 'It will be a happy day', Cobden thought, 'when England has not an acre of territory in Continental Asia.'[27] 'They are doing the people of this country the greatest service who tell them the honest truth according to their convictions, and prepare them for abandoning at some future time the thankless and impossible task.'[28]

But Cobden knew full well that his opinions did not 'harmonize with the views and prejudices of the British public'.[29] In 1853 he had realized 'the difficulty of arousing the attention of the English public' to the wars in India, for they were 'carried on at the expense of the people of India' and were considered to be profitable by all classes in England.³⁰ Nor did the employers, who supported him in his free-trade campaign, agree with him over India. He lamented: 'How few of those who fought for the repeal of the Corn Law, really understand the meaning of Free Trade principles! If you talk to our Lancashire friends they argue that unless we occupied India there would be no trade with that country, or that somebody else would monopolize it, forgetting that this is the old protectionist theory which they used formerly to ridicule. India was a great centre and source of commerce for the civilized world before Englishmen took to wearing breeches, and it was the renown of its wealth and productiveness which first attracted us there. I am by no means so clear as some people, that we have added greatly to its commerce. Certainly the trade of European countries has increased in a greater ratio than that of India during the last century.'³¹ Cobden knew the way the tide of public opinion in England was flowing at the time of the revolt of 1857 in India and considered it fortunate that he was out of Parliament. 'I bless my stars', he wrote, 'that I am not in a position to be obliged to give public utterance to my views on the all-absorbing topic of the day, for I could not do justice to my own convictions and possess the confidence of any constituency in the kingdom. For where do we find even an individual who is not imbued with the notion that England would sink to ruin if she were deprived of her Indian Empire? Leave me, then, to my pigs and sheep, which are not labouring under any such delusion. . . .'³² The revolt suppressed, Cobden was disgusted to find London political circles in 1858 talking only about the chances of turning out one ministry and bringing in another, with 'scarcely a word about the best mode of governing the millions of India'.³³ In March 1858 he had written to a friend: 'What a pretentious and hypocritical people we are in our dealings with the outside world! How we abuse and bully king Bomba because he will not govern his lazzaroni according to our notions of constitutionalism! But when you propose to apply a little of our love of liberty to our own fellow-subjects in India, "oh! oh!" is the reply you meet with in the House. Yet you would have no difficulty in carrying the cheers of the said House for any proposal to put the slaves in America or Cuba immediately on the same political level as their masters. This nation will meet with a terrible check some day, unless it makes a little better progress in the science of self-knowledge.'³⁴

With Bright, too, India was a great problem—the greatest any nation had ever to solve—of politics and morality, which would try all the intelligence and virtue in England. Edmund Burke had called the government of India a 'trust' and remarked: 'There we are, there we are placed by the Sovereign Disposer; and we must do the best in our situation. The situation of man is the preceptor of his duty.'[35] To him India was a moral challenge, a test of national character. So was it with Bright, 'our great and terrible moral responsibility'.[36] India had been acquired by unrighteous means; 'grave errors—if not grievous crimes—had been committed in that country'.[37] Its development had been neglected and its finances squandered. Indians were taxed oppressively. The administration of the country was faulty and expensive. The Indian government often engaged itself in unjustifiable aggressions.[38] Bright wanted all this to change. He demanded a better, juster and more humane government for that country. 'What we want with regard to the government of India', he said in the House of Commons on 24 June 1858, 'is that which in common conversation is called "a little more daylight". We want more simplicity and more responsibility.'[39] The edifice reared in India was too vast and cumbrous. He advocated decentralization, reduction in military expenditure, a conciliatory and moderate government, with sound finances, a union of the government with the governed by means of an increasing association of Indians in administration and legislation. He wished for no mere change in machinery, but 'a new feeling in England, and an entirely new policy in India'.[40] 'The good of England must come through the channels of the good of India.'[41] He strongly condemned racial arrogance on the part of Englishmen and the calumnies uttered against the people of India. Indians had so far known 'England in its worst form in that country' as invader and conqueror. It was for Englishmen to strive assiduously to correct that impression.[42] He invited Parliament 'to a glory not "fanned by conquest's crimson wing", but based upon the solid and lasting benefits'[43] which it could confer upon the people of India. He accepted the possession of India 'as a fact', but added: 'There we are; we do not know how to leave it, and therefore let us see if we know how to govern it.'[44] The people of India were 'sheep literally without a shepherd' who scarcely knew 'where to turn if we left them'.[45] He warned Parliament: 'They are people whom you have subdued, and who have the highest and strongest claims upon you—claims which you cannot forget—claims which, if you do not act upon, you may rely upon it that, if there be a judgment for nations—as I believe there is—as for individuals, our children at no distant generation must pay the penalty which we have purchased by neglecting our duty to the populations of India.'[46]

Bright's interest in India began in the late 1830s and it ceased only with his death. He always remained dissatisfied with the government of that country. It was partly because he considered it to be incorrigible that he refused to take up the secretaryship of India when it was offered to him in 1868.[47] He did not advocate the policy of abandoning India, because it would have been criminal in his eyes to do so in the existing helpless condition of the country,[48] but he continued reminding the English people of their duty and solemn responsibility in India. In 1877 he remarked at Manchester: 'I believe that it is our duty not only to govern India well now for our own sakes and to satisfy our own conscience, but so to arrange its government and so to administer it that we should look forward to the time—which may be distant, but may not be so remote—when India will have to take up her own government, and administer it in her own fashion.' He was 'no statesman', he said, 'no man actuated with a high moral sense', who was 'not willing thus to look ahead, and thus to prepare for circumstances which may come sooner than we think, and sooner than any of us hope for, but which must come at some not very distant date'. In this manner alone, he said, could the British people 'make amends for the original crime upon which much of our power in India is founded, and for the many mistakes which have been made'. It was their duty to strive to give to the people of India 'that good government and that freedom which He, who is supreme over all lands and all peoples, will in His own good time make the possession of all His children'.[49]

Richard Congreve, the most celebrated of the British Comtists, took a keen interest in India. Before 1857 he had contented himself with protesting against the British Indian Empire, but 'accepted it as a fact'.[50] As he wrote in 1857: 'Not blind to the wrong means by which it was acquired, not blind to the inherent evils of its ultimate retention—evil both to England and to India—I had yet hoped that the hour of its fall might be adjourned for some time. And I had rested my hope on the conviction that the English Government, by the enforcement of order, the furtherance of material improvements, and by the lessons of Western punctuality and honour, was in some measure redeeming its origin, and if not in principle justified, was in its practical results offering to its Eastern subjects some perceptible compensation for its conquest. In this feeling I waited patiently for the day when either the energies of the native population should make our further hold impossible, or, what was more desirable; the spread of a purer moral feeling on such subjects should lead the English nation voluntarily to abandon that hold, and of itself retiring from India, after having done everything possible to secure the country it had so long ruled, order, good government, and external security.'[51] But the revolt of 1857 in India dispelled all such ideas and Congreve began to preach that 'we [the British] withdraw from our occupation of India without any unnecessary delay, within the shortest period compatible with due regard for the security of European life and property, and with such measures as shall be deemed advisable in the interests of Indian independence and good government'.[52] In his view, the great object was the British withdrawal from India and the cessation of the British dominion. Though the British had neglected it, their best claim to their position in India had always been as trustees and representatives of the civilization of the west. 'Let us, in the spirit of this claim, secure, as we may easily do, a guarantee on the part of all the great European Powers that the empire we retire from shall not be considered open to the ambition of any of them, and that no extra-European Power shall have a right which we renounce ourselves.'[53] He even suggested the establishment of a mixed commission, similar in principle to the one appointed to investigate the question of the Danubian principalities, consisting of the representatives of France, Portugal, Denmark, Saridinia, Turkey, and Britain, which would 'act in concert with any Government established or to be established in India' and 'settle the terms on which the interchange of the Western world with India could be continued'.[54] This might form the basis of a European protectorate of India, but the objects of British policy should remain: 'the withdrawal of English occupation; the securing the independence of India; the retaining a wholesome commercial and moral connection between the East and the West'.[55]

Congreve believed that, though Britain had occupied India in 'rashness', the spirit she should 'bring to its relinquishment is that of the calmest judgment, of the most absolute self-denial'. 'Like an unskilful physician, we interfered with the course of nature, and suspended its healing action. The confession of this error constitutes a demand for the highest exertion of will in meeting its consequences.'[56] There could be no permanent union between Britain and India. 'Open any map of the world, and see the relative position of the two countries: it constitutes a strong presumption against their union. Then estimate their relative population, their differences of climate, language, religion, manners and customs, and have you not so many additional presumptions? Ask yourself under what conditions a conquest is either justifiable or admissible; and then ask yourself whether in the case of India, any one of these conditions is realized. Treat the question either on moral or political grounds, I have no fear of the answer.'[57]

Congreve did not subscribe to the view that the possession of India added to the strength of Britain or that its retention was necessary for the sake of British commerce. Britain's commercial intercourse with India existed even before India was conquered, and it would continue to exist after her withdrawal. As the example of the United States of America showed, Britain's commerce was as profitable or even more so with an independent or actually hostile country as with one that was dependent.[58] India was not a source of strength to Britain, but a source of political weakness. What would have happened if the revolt of 1857 in India had come when England was engaged in a war with Russia. 'No! the cry for colonies or dependencies is at any rate a delusion, so far as it is thought that they increase our strength. They are incumbrances on our finances, and a drain on our military power. We are great, not by virtue of them, but in spite of them; they are burdensome outworks, from which we should retire for concentration. We were great when no dream of Indian acquisitions had occupied any adventurer. We should be great again, when the energies of the nation shall have a great government to give them a wholesome direction, a noble expression.'[59]

The plea that England held India for the sake of civilization and that released from the English hold India would fall into disorder and barbarism, carried no weight with Congreve, because, as he wrote: 'I have gained a respect for that ancient polytheistic civilization with which our own social order is but a child in point of duration.'⁶⁰ He even deemed it 'unwise to press on India the adoption of the progressive, yet still anarchical civilization of the West'.⁶¹

Congreve not only did not see any hope of Indians accepting Christianity in large numbers in the foreseeable future, he was even inclined to think 'that it would be, not a gain, but a loss to the Hindoo nation, were it persuaded to accept Christianity'.⁶²

Congreve believed that England's original title to be in India was bad, her subsequent government had not been wholly defensible, and her ultimate tenure was uncertain at the best. 'More distant than ever will be the day of our leaving, if it is left to us to judge the proper moment.'⁶³ It was certain that sooner or later India would be torn from England. She should, therefore, clearly indicate the probable date of her withdrawal, for 'the only real glory she can hope to gain by India is by its voluntary restitution to its inhabitants'.⁶⁴

Congreve, however, had no illusions about the reception of his ideas in England. He knew that he was arguing 'in support of a line of policy alien in conception and results to the thoughts and wishes of the upper classes of England'.⁶⁵ 'I am aware', he wrote, 'that I stand in comparative isolation.... But as I hope for no immediate acceptance, in my country or time, of such political doctrines as I have expressed, so in the future I am confident of their prevalence.'⁶⁶

When after the suppression of the Indian revolt of 1857-9, the British government ordered the Thanksgiving for 1 May 1859, Congreve publicly protested against it, 'believeing the cause of the English in India to be unjust, that of the Hindoo just, as the legitimate efforts of a nation to shake off an oppressive foreign yoke; believing, consequently, the English success to be the triumph of force over right'.⁶⁷

Congreve continued to hold these views in later years. In 1872 he reprinted without any alterations his pamphlet *India* written in 1857. In the same year he reflected on the 'Moral and Social Questions Connected with our Indian Empire', and remarked that the Indian revenue vitiated England's intercourse with China; it acted as an oppressive weight on her European policy; it warped the views of many in England and controlled the action of the British government in regard to Gibraltar (which, he advocated, should be returned to Spain). Congreve reiterated his view that England's tenure was uncertain in duration and that it was bound to end in ultimate failure unless she obviated the failure by wise retirement.[68]

The great Indian nationalist leader Dadabhai Naoroji made the following entry in his diary after meeting with Congreve in London on 15 April 1886; 'Called at Dr. R. Congreve's .... He thought the connexion between England and India should be severed; it was injuring England; it was doing harm to the whole English character .... I was of a different opinion that the connexion should continue for the sake of India and that if certain reforms, which were sorely needed by India, were made, the connexion would be a blessing to both. I stated about Poverty and the remedy of the substitution of Native agency. This, he said, was just the thing which the statesmen would not dare to do. The English agency in India is an immediate benefit and they would not give it up. ... A separation must come in time when the people generally are sufficiently advanced for self-government and political knowledge. Statesmen like Salisbury and Hartington were, he said, afraid of this very thing, that Ireland being separated, India would come next for something similar, and this they consider the destruction of the Empire.'[69]

Dilke was probably more interested in India than in the self-governing colonies. In his *Greater Britain* (1868) he argued that the retention of the colonies did not pay, but this was, in his view, not true of India and the other dependencies. We have already noted his views about the necessity of keeping the British flag flying in India if trade with that country was to continue. Further, the dependencies formed 'a nursery of statesmen and warriors' and England would 'irresistibly fall into national sluggishness of thought' were she not required to govern and educate the inhabitants of backward countries.[70] 'The possession of India', he wrote, 'offers to ourselves that element of vastness of dominion which, in this age, is needed to secure width of thought and nobility of purpose. ...'[71]

Dilke believed that as India could not within a reasonable future govern herself, England must govern her 'in the interests of the people of Hindostan'.[72] England's mission in the East was 'to plant free institutions among dark-skinned races'.[73] 'The only justification for our presence in India', wrote Dilke, 'is the education for freedom of the Indian races.'[74]

Dilke found fault with 'our somewhat blind love for "progress" '[75] and 'our levelling rule'[76] in India, which had humbled the old upper classes without raising a new middle class to take its place. British rule in India was 'the best example of a well-administered despotism',[77] but its 'one great fault' was over-centralization,[78] and its tendency was 'to become an imperialism, or despotism exercised over a democratic people such as we see in France, and are commencing to see in Russia'.[79] The British government in India was too rigidly western and suffered from lack of adaptability and elasticity. It was unacquainted with the feelings of the people and lamentably ignorant about the facts of their life.[80] It had created a numerous class of educated Indians, but offered them no chance of any but subordinate career. This not only created discontent but enfeebled Indian character. 'That such men as Madhava Rao and Salar Jung should be unable to find suitable employment in our service is one of the standing reproaches of our rule.'[81] He strongly advocated the increased employment of Indians in all services and greater encouragement of the English language. The great advantage of the latter, he said, would be that 'its acquisition by the Hindoos will soon place the government of India in native hands, and thus, gradually relieving us of an almost intolerable burthen, will civilize and set free the people of Hindostan'.[82]

'If India is to be governed by the British race at all,' Dilke insisted, 'it must be governed from Great Britain. The general conditions of our rule must be dictated at London by the English people, and nothing but the execution of our decrees, the collection of evidence, and the framing of mere rules, left to our subordinates in the East.'[83] For Dilke was of the opinion that 'India, as a whole,' was 'far better understood in England than in any presidency town'.[84]

Dilke believed that the presence of the British in India for the time being was justifiable. Were they to quit India, they would leave her to Russia or to herself. A Russian occupation of India, besides being a blow to British prestige and trade, would be a disaster for the people of India themselves, for the Russians were, according to him, a barbarous horde who would surpass even eastern tyrants in corruption, cruelty and oppression. If India were to be left to herself, 'unextinguishable anarchy would involve our Eastern trade and India's happiness in a hideous and lasting ruin'.[85] But English rule should gradually prepare the Indian people for freedom. Dilke did not believe that self-government could only exist where the snow would lie deep upon the ground and that despotism followed the palm-belt round the world. 'If freedom be good in one country,' he wrote, 'it is good in all, for there is nothing in its essence which should limit it in time or place....'[86] 'We should know that the Sikhs, Kandians, Scindians, Marattas, have fought bravely enough for national independence to make it plain that they will struggle to the death for liberty as soon as they can be made to see its worth. It will take years to efface the stain of a couple of hundred years of slavery in the negroes of America, and it may take scores of years to heal the deeper sores of Hindostan; but history teaches us to believe that the time will come when the Indians will be fit for freedom.'[87]

India was fast changing, noted Dilke, a nation was being made out of what was ten years ago but a continent inhabited by an agglomeration of distinct tribes, and no Anglo-Indian who left India for ten years was competent even to advise, much less to share, in the government of that country.[88] In a memorable passage in *Greater Britain* we read: 'The greatest of the many changes in progress in the East is that India is being made—that a country is being created under that name where none has yet existed; and it is our railroads, our annexations, and above all our centralizing policy, that are doing the work. There is no reason to fear that this change will be hastened by the extension of our new codes to the former "non-regulation provinces", and by government from at home, where India is looked upon as one nation, instead of from Calcutta, where it is known to be still composed of fifty; but so rapid is the change, that already the Calcutta people are mistaken in attempting to laugh down our phrase "the people of India", as we were during the mutiny, when we believed that there was an "India" writhing in our clutches. Whether the India which is being thus rapidly built up by our own hands will be friendly to us, or the reverse, depends upon ourselves.'[89] The British people, he wrote, had rejected the principle of holding India for the sake of prestige and trade and deliberately decided 'to govern India in the interest of the people of Hindostan' and the task of statesmanship was to think out methods by which this accepted principle was to be worked out.⁹⁰ And Dilke prophesied: 'If, when India has passed through the present transition stage from a country of many peoples to a country of only one, we cannot continue to rule her by the consent of the majority of her inhabitants, our occupation of the country must come to an end, whether we will or no.'⁹¹

The views expressed by Cobden, Bright, Congreve, and Dilke about India have a sort of family likeness to those expressed by the other contemporary anti-imperialists who confined their attention mainly to the self-governing colonies. This likeness is better appreciated if due allowance is made for the peculiar position of India in the British Empire and the circumstances prevailing in that country at the time. The arguments used by the mid-Victorian anti-imperialists differed, but their message was the same. They were all trying, in effect, to tell their fellow-countrymen this: the Empire is changing and cannot last for ever; it is not an end in itself, but a means to an end; think nobly but realistically about it.

4

IMPERIAL FEDERATION AND INDIA, 1868-1917

The Early Federationists and India

'When we inquire then into the Greater Britain of the future', observed Seeley in 1883, 'we ought to think much more of our Colonial than of our Indian Empire.'[1] Those who, like Seeley, busied themselves with the problems of imperial unity in the last third of the nineteenth century did think much more of the 'Colonial' than of the 'Indian Empire'. They were mainly concerned about the possibility of a closer union between Great Britain and the self-governing colonies and paid comparatively little attention to India. Freeman wrote in 1885 of the imperial federationists of his day that in their argument 'India, so present to every mind in every other argument, India, the choicest flower of the Empire, the brightest jewel in the Imperial Crown—any other figure of speech that may spring of the oriental richness of an imperial fancy—seems suddenly to be forgotton'.[2] Sir Charles Dilke accused the advocates of imperial federation of the same lapse in 1892.[3] And the journal of the Imperial Federation League admitted in December 1893 that India had been 'commonly ignored' by them.[4]

The reasons why India was 'forgotten' or 'ignored' by the early federationists are not far to seek. She was quiet and securely in hand. Her problems were problems of administration and not those demanding a change in her connexion with Great Britain. The white colonies were rapidly advancing in self-government and nationhood and it was widely felt that unless some positive effort was made to draw them closer to the mother country they would drift into sovereign independence. The immediate challenge came from the self-governing colonies; the problem of determining future relations with them was the urgent one. India posed no such pressing problem. 'Federate or disintegrate' could not be said of the British Empire in India.

The so-called anti-imperialists of the fifties and sixties of the nineteenth century had concentrated mainly on the self-governing colonies, for they 'offered an easier target for their arguments than the possessions proper',[5] and, naturally enough, the new imperialism, which began almost as a protest and reaction against separatist views, tended to move in the selfsame groove.

The great aim of the federationists was 'to reunite the scattered fragments of the same nation'.[6] Their conception of the Empire was frankly racial. With a few exceptions,[7] they either neglected India altogether or expressly excluded her from their schemes of closer union on the ground that her inhabitants were 'not of the British race'.[8]

Suggestions for a federation of the self-governing portions of the Empire, having a community of race, religion, language and culture, had at least an air of plausibility about them. India was not self-governing. She was not a 'colony' in the strict sense of the term, but a foreign 'dependency'. She was held not by the bonds of affection but 'by the sword'. A federal relationship with India was obviously absurd and unthinkable. The imperial federationists may, therefore, be excused if they did not take her into account whilst framing their schemes of 'Britannic Confederation' or shut her out on the ground that she had no representative government.[9]

India was not only alien and dependent, she was multitudinous, and there were many who feared that her representation in an 'Imperial Parliament' would be neither easy nor safe.

Dreamers though they were, the federationists could not remain wholly oblivious of the immense difficulties in the way of the realization of their dream. They were naturally anxious not to add to those difficulties by bringing in the question of India. 'The question of federating the British Empire', said Frederick Young, was 'already complicated enough'. Why should we, he asked, 'further complicate' it by taking up the question of India's inclusion 'now'?[10] 'Some means might perhaps ultimately be devised for giving India representation in the Federal Parliament', remarked another ardent federationist, F. P. de Labilliere; but he asserted that 'the possibility or impossibility of making India a member of our Imperial Federation ought not for one moment to retard the Federal union of our British fellow-countrymen in these isles and beyond the seas'.[11]

While the imperial federation movement claimed the adherence of quite a few men prominent in the public life of the mother country and the colonies, its ranks were conspicuous by the absence of any well-known Anglo-Indian.[12] This may also partly account for the fact that the movement remained preoccupied with what was called 'the colonial question'.

There was yet another reason why India figured so rarely in the proposals of the federationists for the reconstruction of the Empire. One of their primary objectives was to persuade the self-governing colonies to share in the ever-increasing defence liabilities of the Empire and lower their tariffs to British manufactures. India had already been shaped nearer to the heart's desire. She paid for her defence and maintained a large British army which could, in emergency, be employed for imperial purposes abroad. She was a free-trade country and took roughly three-fourths of her imports from Great Britain. India left little more to be desired from the federationists' point of view and was therefore neglected by them.

The Problem of the Indian Empire

Their critics did not fail to detect this chink in the armour of the federationists. A parliament of the Empire without any representatives of the vast population of India, H.B.T. Strangways told a meeting of the Royal Colonial Institute in 1880, would be 'something like *Hamlet* with Hamlet left out'.[13] 'The Imperial state of all, that Empire of India set alone in its august rank above the mere kingdoms of lowlier Europe', said Freeman, was 'the head and front of the Imperial power of Britain'.[14] 'Does Imperial Federation take in India or not?',[15] he asked. And he pointed out that if the empire of India were to be excluded, the federation could hardly deserve to be called imperial. If, on the other hand, India were to be taken in, she would by her mere size and numbers overwhelm and outvote the other parts of the federation—a prospect which, he said, no one would contemplate for a moment. Nor would this be a move in the direction of imperialism, for if dominion over India were exchanged for a federal union with her the 'empire' would disappear. 'The simple truth is', Freeman concluded, 'that the phrase "Imperial Federation" is a contradiction in terms, that what is imperial cannot be federal, and what is federal cannot be imperial.'[16] The Radical Australian *Bulletin* pointed out that any scheme of imperial federation worthy of the name would have to include India, in which case she would dominate the rest of the Empire; if, on the other hand, India were excluded, the federation would be merely 'a league of the conquerors for the more effectual subjugation of the conquered'.[17]

To the cry of the sceptics, 'But above all, what is to be done with India?',[18] the zealots replied that she was no problem at all, for either the federal government of the Empire could undertake her government or England alone could continue to remain responsible for it.[19] But neither of these two courses was free from objections. 'Have the colonists the leisure and the special competency to take part in the governance of India? Will they pay for the defence of the Indian frontiers?', Morley had asked in 1884.[20] If India were to be governed, said Goldwin Smith, by a federation of democratic communities scattered over the globe, some of whom, like Canada, having no interest in her whatever, her 'fate as an empire would then be sealed, if it is not sealed already by the progress of democracy in Great Britain'.[21] If India were to continue being governed by England alone, then, he pointed out, one member of the federation would have an empire five times as large as the rest of the federation, requiring separate defence liabilities and diplomacy.[22]

Avowed anti-federationists, like Freeman and Goldwin Smith, tried to make India 'the crux of the Federation problem'[23] solely to embarrass their opponents and to score a debating point. The federationists could therefore afford to neglect them. But they could not similarly treat those who, while apparently sympathizing with their aspirations, objected to India's exclusion on the ground that without her the federation would be lame. 'Her [India's] 280 millions', wrote the *Asiatic Quarterly Review*, 'cannot be omitted from any rational plan of Confederation; and it is childish to discuss schemes which leave out of consideration so important a component of the British Empire.'[24] The journal condemned the proposal to restrict federation to the self-governing colonies as 'absurd, meaningless and impossible'[25] and remarked that India was 'perhaps even more important to our Empire than any, if not all, of the Colonies'.²⁶

India loomed large in the imagination of the British. Rightly or wrongly, they ascribed their power, prestige and prosperity to the possession of that vast and glorious dependency. She was, in a sense, dearer to the hearts of most Englishmen than even the daughter nations. Federationists, like the colonial Labilliere,²⁷ might complain that the worth of India was overesteemed in England, but they had to take this fact into account.

That the problem of India was a serious complication was admitted by one of the foremost champions of closer union. G.R. Parkin wrote in 1892: 'The political difficulty about India's relation to a united Empire is ... felt very widely. It is one of the first which occurs to the minds of most men when they turn their attention to the question, as I have found during public discussions in many parts of the Empire.'²⁸

Persistent criticism by friends and foes alike, a desire to make their proposals comprehensive and theoretically perfect, and the recognition that India was too important a part of the Empire to be neglected, compelled an increasing number of federationists, from the latter half of the 'eighties onwards, to attempt to provide for the inclusion of India in their schemes of imperial reorganization.²⁹ This trend was reinforced by the remark made by Lord Salisbury in his reply to a deputation of the Imperial Federation League in June 1891, that the formation of 'a *Kriegsverein* means some control of foreign policy: a common control of foreign policy means balance and appraisement of the voting value of the various elements of which the Empire is composed, and when you come to tot up that calculation you cannot leave our Asiatic dependencies out of sight'.³⁰

As more and more federation-enthusiasts, despairing of the prospect of a real federation, directed their attention to the more practical problems of imperial co-operation in defence and trade, they recognized the value of India to the Empire. India conformed, however unwillingly, to the free trade orthodoxy. Her army of 75,000 British and 160,000 native troops—supplemented by the Imperial Service Corps, numbering 20,000, voluntarily raised by the Indian princes—was the second right arm of Britain. It began to be argued by a section of federationists, who believed in free trade and in combining the resources of the Empire for common defence, that India had 'advanced further towards Imperial Federation than any other part of the British Empire'[31] and that 'India alone takes already its right place in Imperial Federation'.[32] India paid for everything she received; she was virtually federated for commerce and for defence with Britain. The colonies, so the argument ran, got much but gave nothing in return; they discriminated against British goods and boasted of their freedom to come and go as they pleased. 'While colonists of Anglo-Saxon blood', complained the *Asiatic Quarterly Review* bitterly, 'impotently swagger about an independence which they are powerless singly to maintain, India, at a month's notice, can even now lend 50,000 splendid troops, to fight England's battle anywhere in the world.'[33] With a singular lack of tact, the *Review* referred the good behaviour of India to the errant colonies as a model to be followed: 'Australia, Canada, and all other dependencies of the Empire should, like India, maintain their own armies, navies, and reserves, ready to answer the call of the Central Government.'[34]

India and Imperial Preference

The Colonial Conferences of 1897 and 1902 had convinced Joseph Chamberlain that the colonies were prepared neither for a political federation, nor, so to speak, to follow India in the matter of free trade and the provision of armed forces which constituted effective components of an imperial reserve. He therefore changed his front and sought to promote imperial unity, as the colonies desired, by means of preferential tariffs. But, either because he had been accustomed to look at the Empire from the narrow window of the Colonial Office, or because he was in such a hurry to forge new bonds of union, Chamberlain completely forgot India when he launched his tariff reform campaign in 1903. His mistake was at once detected not only by his Liberal critics but also by members of his own party, men like Lord George Hamilton and Curzon, who were avowed 'imperialists'. Three of the four living ex-viceroys and all the living preceding secretaries of state for India denounced Chamberlain's policy. Hamilton resigned in protest. Curzon considered Chamberlain to be 'Colony-mad'[35] and accused him of failing to take into account the 'largest and most powerful unit' of the Empire.[36] The government of India sent home a dispatch in October 1903, containing a reasoned and strongly-worded protest against any scheme of preferential tariffs.[37] The dispatch became a thorn in the side of the tariff reformers.

Chamberlain's neglect of India had at least one good result. It provoked a widespread discussion of India's value to the Empire, and a demand, from various quarters, that she should be adequately represented at the 'Imperial Conference'. India's partial representation at the Colonial Conference of 1907 was, in a sense, due to this agitation.

The Government of India and the 'Imperial Conference'

India was Britain's best customer and the pivot of her imperial policy. No organization which dealt with the problems of imperial defence and trade—as the Colonial Conference increasingly tended to do—could afford to neglect her. And the governors of India saw to it that she was not neglected. They had shown little interest in the amateurish and vague schemes of imperial federation of the earlier era, but as the Colonial Conference established itself as the regular deliberative assembly of the Empire, Indian officials were the first to demand that the voice of India should not remain unheard. Conscious of their own importance as the rulers over millions of men and of India's great position in the Empire, they resented their exclusion from a place 'at the "high table" in the banquet hall of the Empire states'.[38] Nor were they unmindful of their responsibilities to India. The government of India had a long-standing dispute with the home government over what it considered to be an unfair burden of military expenditure imposed on India and an unjust interference by the latter with Indian tariffs. Only recently, in 1903, it had resisted successfully a War Office attempt to make India pay for the garrisons in South Africa. We have already noted the determined opposition which it offered to the schemes of preferential tariffs within the Empire, as being inimical to Indian interests. As the guardian of Indian interests in trade and finance, the government of India demanded representation at the 'Imperial Conference'. The vexed question of Indian immigrants in the dominions—over which the government of India made common cause with Indian nationalists—provided an additional argument in favour of such representation. The realities of responsive government in India, like the realities of responsible government in the dominions, pointed not in the direction of imperial federation but away from it.

'The Two Empires'[39]

The great debate in the last quarter of the nineteenth century about the future reorganization of the Empire brought into bolder relief the idea that the Empire was constituted of two disparate elements: the one white and self-governing, the other non-white and dependent. The former was 'Greater Britain', an 'expansion of England', 'the sphere of settlement', 'an empire of dwelling places'; it was not really 'empire' in the strict sense of the term but a 'commonwealth'. The latter belonged to 'the sphere of rule', the English were in it but not of it; it was the true 'empire' in the classic continental tradition.

Early in the present century this concept of 'the two empires' was underlined by those who were eager for a readjustment of relations between the mother country and the self-governing colonies. The two different and contrasted units of the Empire, they argued, demanded different treatment. They advocated the policy of union and partnership with regard to 'the self-governing Empire' and that of retention and profitable development with regard to 'the dependent Empire'.[40] Some of them were even inclined to think that a basis for imperial partnership between the self-governing parts of the Empire could be found in their joint guardianship of the dependencies. Richard Jebb, for example, though he was an autonomist and not a federationist, thought that 'the dependencies of England themselves may supply the organic link, uniting the mother country with the daughter states in an Imperial partnership adapted for carrying on the work of administering the subject countries'.[41] He believed that the colonies were ripe for 'Roman imperialism', 'the imperialism of the "White Man's Burden"', and suggested that Britain should invite their assistance in administering India.[42] The same idea was advocated by L.S. Amery,[43] Milner,[44] and others. They insisted that a beginning in this direction should be made by appointing colonials to the Indian Civil Service.[45] The impracticability of their recommendation was, however, exposed when Morley, as secretary of state for India, communicated to Minto, the viceroy, the suggestion of Albert Grey, the governor-general of Canada and an ardent imperial federationist, that a few posts should be found in the I.C.S. for Rhodes scholars.[46] Minto replied that appointments to the I.C.S. were by competition and any advantage to candidates from the colonies would be extremely unpopular in India, where their policies of racial discrimination were resented. Minto also warned the secretary of state that the acceptance of Grey's proposal would reopen the old question of the possibility of simultaneous examinations for the I.C.S. in England and in India.[47]

Nor did appeals to 'take up the White Man's Burden' in India evoke any sympathetic response in the dominions. Young men in the dominions had never shown any marked desire to serve in India. They had little of 'the Imperial—the ruling instinct'[48] which romantic imperialists in the mother country were so eager to gratify.

The Round Table Group and India[49]

When the Round Table group[50] took up the cause of imperial federation in 1909, it thought primarily in terms of an organic union between Great Britain and the self-governing colonies. It envisaged a federal imperial parliament, consisting of representatives from the mother country and the dominions, and responsible for defence, foreign affairs and the government of large dependencies like India—responsibility for the last being considered inseparable from that for the first two. The group began with the traditional asumption—shared by most British Tories and Liberals of the day—that oriental communities were incapable of governing themselves and would remain so for a long, long time to come. It invited the people of the dominions to share in the heavy imperial burden of the mother country and chided them for their ignorance of and indifference to the subject millions committed as a solemn trust to the British race. But the group had not proceeded very far in its inquiries when it was confronted with the awkward problem of India. In the summer of 1912 three of its prominent members —Philip Kerr,[51] Sir James Meston[52] and William Marris[53]— urged that India should be allotted a few seats in the projected imperial parliament. The arguments which they advanced in support of their proposal were as follows:

The problem of India is unique and demands special treatment. India cannot be dismissed under the label 'dependency', for she is the Empire. She is Britain's greatest economic and military asset. Her vast population of 300 millions—three-fourths of the total population of the Empire—contains a fair number of men who are as educated, cultured and loyal as any in other parts of the

Empire. India cannot be transferred like an inert mass into the new imperial organization. She has a vocal public opinion which will have to be taken into account. Indians will demand—have in fact already demanded—representation at the imperial parliament and it will be impossible to say 'no' to them. They will plead their military contribution to the Empire and the need for being placed in a position to be able to counteract what they consider to be the evil influence of ignorant and hostile colonials; they will invoke the solemn pledges of equal rights and privileges repeatedly given to them in the past. Their demand will be supported by liberal opinion at home. Indians will strenuously resist their subordination to a legislature containing colonials. On whatever ground it is done, Indians will interpret their exclusion from the imperial parliament as being motivated by racial prejudice. It will wound their *amour propre* and shake their faith in the good intentions of Britain. It will cause extreme bitterness which will not only add to the difficulties of Indian administration, but also prompt Indians to seek their destiny outside the British Empire. The declared policy of the British government is to associate more and more Indians with the administration and to increase their representation on the local legislative councils; the admission of two or three Indians to the imperial parliament will be merely an extension of this wise and liberal policy.[54]

Kerr, Marris and Meston did not restrict themselves to a plea for India's representation at the imperial parliament. They went on to argue that self-government was the only intelligible goal of British policy in India and to demand that Britain should explicitly recognize this goal and try to develop India on the lines of the self-governing dominions.[55]

This attempt to get the Round Table to revise its original stand on India was resisted by a minority in the group, chief amongst whom were G. L. Craik[56] and D. O. Malcolm.[57] They argued that as India was not self-governing—and would not be so for generations to come—she could not be represented at the imperial parliament. They even doubted whether it would be wise to have India in the British Empire when—if ever—she was self-governing. Their main objection, however, to the admission of Indians to the imperial parliament was that it would make the federal scheme totally unacceptable to the dominions.[58]

Lionel Curtis,[59] 'the Prophet' of the group, favoured the presence of a few Indians in the imperial parliament as assessors, in order to acquaint the real rulers of India with the Indian point of view. But he maintained that as long as India was not self-governing she could not be really 'represented' at the imperial parliament. To invite Indians to share in the government of the Empire while they were not yet responsible for their own internal government would be, he argued, a violation of the fundamental principle of the federation; it would also be impolitic, for it would create a wrong impression in the minds of Indians that their country was ripe for self-government when in fact it was not—there being no genuine electorates even for a province or district.[60]

But, while Curtis opposed the proposal of Kerr, Marris and Meston for India's immediate and special representation at the imperial parliament, he had already been converted to their view that ultimate self-government for India should be the goal of British policy. He had abandoned his earlier belief that self-government was a principle of western life alone and come to recognize that it was a principle valid for all peoples. He incorporated this new outlook in the doctrine of the commonwealth which he formulated in 1912. 'For a commonwealth', wrote Curtis, 'to govern communities not deemed as [sic] included in its citizenship is to violate its own essential principles.'[61] He argued that a commonwealth governing a dependency without having as its main object the training of the inhabitants of that dependency up to the status of citizens in order to enable them to assume the full rights and duties of citizenship, was acting like a despot and proving itself false to the law of its being. He pleaded that 'Indians should be regarded as fellow-citizens of one super-commonwealth with ourselves, and that to prepare them first for the control of their sub-commonwealth and finally for an equal share in the control of the super-commonwealth should be our guiding principle'.[62]

This doctrine of the commonwealth in itself—leaving aside its federalist overtones—represented almost a revolution in imperial thinking.[63] It repudiated the concept of 'the two empires'—the concept that there could be under the British flag one form of constitutional evolution for the west and another for the east, or one for the white races and another for the non-white. It affirmed that to prepare for self-government those peoples in the Empire who were as yet incapable of governing themselves was the supreme duty of the Empire, the spiritual end for which it existed.

The Round Table group decided in 1912 to leave the question of India's status in the Empire to be settled by the reconstructed imperial parliament itself. Most of its members, including Curtis, thought that the mutual relations of Great Britain and the dominions—the self-governing parts of the Empire—should be adjusted first, and that the problem of India, being less urgent and more difficult, could wait. This was, however, soon proved to be a mistaken assumption.

In August 1914 came the war. India's splendid rally to the cause of the Empire strengthened her claim for admission to its inner circle and persuaded even the most conservative imperialist in Britain to view the problems of her internal development and place in the Empire from a changed angle. Indian nationalists welcomed the idea of imperial federation, but they demanded that India must have 'home rule' first and a status similar to that of the dominions in the federation. They registered an emphatic protest against the suggestion that their country might be subordinated to an imperial parliament which included representatives from the dominions. In September 1915 a non-official resolution was introduced into the Indian legislative council, asking that India should be directly represented at the next Imperial Conference, to which the British government gave a friendly reply.

All these developments convinced the Round Table group that India would have to be granted representation in the imperial parliament. But if India was to be granted representation in the imperial parliament, it was necessary to determine whether (and, if so, to what extent and in what form) the beginning of responsible government would be practicable in India itself in the near future. The inquiry conducted by the group for this purpose produced a method of introducing and gradually extending responsible government in India, which was later nicknamed 'dyarchy' and became the basis of the Montagu-Chelmsford reforms.

The imperial federation—'the super-commonwealth'—visualized by the Round Table failed to materialize, but its concept of 'India within the commonwealth' and of the British Empire as 'the project of a commonwealth' of nations, was embodied in the decisions of the British government in 1917. In April of that year India was admitted to the full membership of the Imperial Conference, and in an historic announcement made four months later the British government explicitly committed itself to the policy of 'progressive realisation of responsible government in India'.[64] The part played by the Round Table in the making of the decisions of 1917 and in the further stages of the reforms in India was certainly significant, if not decisive.

In seeking a solution of the difficult problem of India's place in an imperial federation, the Round Table group was led not only into enunciating the principle but also into laying the foundations of our present multi-racial Commonwealth. 'If we manage to create in India a self-governing, responsible dominion,' Philip Kerr had told a Tronto audience in July 1912, 'and if India, when it is responsible and self-governing, elects to remain within the British Empire, we shall have solved the greatest difficulty which presents itself to the world to-day.'[65] The greatest difficulty of which Philip Kerr spoke—that of reconciling east and west and black and white—still remains with us, but the British Commonwealth represents the most hopeful experiment in solving it, and history will not fail to give credit to the Round Table group of federationists for their part in launching that experiment.

5

INDIA'S REPRESENTATION AT THE IMPERIAL CONFERENCE

The first Colonial Conference held in 1887, the year of Queen Victoria's Jubilee celebrations, was a rather casual and motley gathering of 121 delegates, representing the United Kingdom, the self-governing colonies, the crown colonies, and the protectorates. India was not represented at it, though the secretary of state for India, Lord Cross, attended its formal opening session.[1] Apparently because the Conference did not include any representative of the British Empire in India, it was officially designated 'Colonial' and not 'Imperial'.[2]

The second Colonial Conference, in 1897, was restricted to the representatives of the mother country and the self-governing colonies. It was—as its official designation suggested—'a Conference between the Secretary of State for the Colonies and the Premiers of the Self-Governing Colonies'.[3] India was thus again excluded, but this did not prevent her becoming a subject of discussion at the Conference. In his opening address to the Conference, the colonial secretary, Joseph Chamberlain, while sympathizing with the determination of the colonies to check the influx of 'people alien in civilization, alien in religion, alien in custom', made an impassioned appeal to them to frame their immigration restriction legislation in such a manner as not to offend 'the traditions of the Empire, which makes no distinction in favour of, or against race or colour', and the susceptibilities of Her Majesty's Indian subjects. 'The United Kingdom owns', he remarked, 'as its brightest and greatest dependency that enormous Empire of India, with 300,000,000 of subjects, who are as loyal to the Crown as you are yourselves, and among them there are hundreds of thousands of men who are every whit as civilized as we are ourselves, who are, if that is anything, better born in the sense that they have older traditions and older families, who are men of wealth, men of cultivation, men of distinguished valour, men who have brought whole armies and placed them at the service of the Queen, and have in time of great difficulty and trouble, such for instance as on the occasion of the Indian Mutiny, saved the Empire by their loyalty. I say, you, who have seen this, cannot be willing to put upon these men slight which I think is absolutely unnecessary for your purpose, and which would be unpalatable to the feelings not only of her Majesty the Queen, but of all her people.'[4] When the Conference took up the question of 'alien immigration' on the fifth and final day of its sittings—8 July 1897—Chamberlain repeated his appeal 'to see that nothing is done unnecessarily offensive or injurious to our Indian fellow subjects' and suggested that the other colonies should at least modify their legislation on the lines of that of Natal, which, though not quite satisfactory to Indians, did 'avoid stigmatizing them by name as being unfit for civilized life'.[5] His appeal, however, fell on deaf ears and he could do little else except express his regret at colonial stubbornness.[6]

We learn of another interesting fact from the confidential report of the 1897 Conference. On the last day of its meeting— 'alien immigration' and 'naval contribution' were the only subjects discussed that day—Sir James Mackay, the financial secretary at the India Office, attended the Conference as one of the private secretaries to Chamberlain, though he did not take part in the discussion.[7]

Before the meeting of the third Colonial Conference in 1902, which was to be like the second 'a Conference between the Secretary of State for the Colonies and the Prime Ministers of Self-Governing Colonies',[8] it was known that one of the principal items on its agenda was the question of a preferential tariff within the British Empire. The Bengal Chamber of Commerce, Calcutta —an influential organization of British commercial interests in India—urged that, in view of the importance of the subject to be discussed, India should be represented at the forthcoming Conference.[9] The government of India under Lord Curzon and the secretary of state for India, Lord George Hamilton, backed their demand.[10] The secretary of state for the colonies, Joseph Chamberlain, agreed, for his ultimate aim was free trade within the Empire and he desired that any preliminary arrangement made at the next Conference should be as comprehensive as possible.[11] 'A representative of the India Office', T.W. Holderness, accordingly, attended the meetings of the Colonial Conference in 1902.[12] Thus began, like so many things British, in a rather casual and unobtrusive manner, the representation of India at the 'Imperial' Conference. Holderness was present at the Conference of 1902 not merely as an observer from a sister department of the state, but also as a watchdog of 'Indian interests'. Far more significant, however, was the mere fact of his presence. It created a precedent for India's representation at the 'Imperial' Conference whenever matters interesting and affecting her were under discussion. When in March 1907 the India Office wrote to the Colonial Office suggesting that arrangements be made for the attendance of its representative at the forthcoming Conference 'as a normal thing', for 'India is really interested in nearly all the questions which will be considered this time', it quoted effectively the precedent of 1902.[13]

The resolutions of the 1902 Conference in regard to preferential tariffs within the Empire were duly communicated to the government of India, who expressed themselves resolutely opposed to the idea. Their objections—contained in a strongly-worded but reasoned dispatch to the secretary of state for India, which was published[14]—provided additional ammunition to Chamberlain's opponents when he launched his tariff reform campaign in late 1903. Writing privately to the secretary of state for India on 24 June 1903, Curzon remarked: 'Chamberlain always seems to me Colony-mad. He is much more concerned with the $10\frac{1}{2}$ millions of white men (by no means the pick of the race) who inhabit those territories than with the 41 millions of the British Isles, or the 300 millions of our subjects in India.'[15] In another communication to Lord Northbrook, dated 12 August 1903, Curzon wrote of Chamberlain: 'I often wonder what would have become of him [Chamberlain] and us, if he had ever visited India. He would have become the greatest Indian Imperialist of the time. The Colonies would have been dwarfed and forgotten; and the pivot of the Empire would have been Calcutta. Not having enjoyed this good fortune, we are now forgotten, and the Empire is to be bound together (or, as we are told, if the prescription is not taken, destroyod) without apparent reference to the requirements of its largest and most powerful unit.'¹⁶ India figured prominently in the tariff reform controversy. The free traders accused Chamberlain of failing to take India into account. They emphasized the value of India and of Indian trade—equal to that of all the self-governing colonies put together—to Great Britain. They painted in lurid colour the grave economic and political consequences which might follow in India an abandonment of the free trade system by Britain. The demand arose from various quarters that India should be adequately represented at the 'Imperial' Conference. It was argued that no organization which dealt with matters concerning imperial defence and trade could afford to neglect India, which was Britain's best customer, the pivot of her defensive system and her greatest military asset.

An informal but influential group in Britain, who were busy examining the problem of imperial reorganization at the time and for whom Sir Frederick Pollock, an eminent jurist, acted as spokesman, recommended that India should be represented at future Conferences by her secretary of state.[17] The council of the British Empire League passed a resolution to the same effect in July 1905.[18] The *British Empire Review* went even further. It protested 'emphatically' against the suggestion that India could be 'sufficiently represented' by her secretary of state alone. 'The day has gone by', it wrote, 'when the right of India to direct representation in an Imperial Council, both in her own interests and in those of the Empire, can be ignored, or the most august of the outlying possessions of the Crown continue to be treated on the level of a Crown Colony.'[18]

Alfred Lyttelton, the successor of Chamberlain at the Colonial Office, was probably one of the undisclosed members of the Pollock group. At any rate, the influence of their proposals is clearly shown in his dispatch of 20 April 1905 to the self-governing colonies, containing suggestions as to 'the future organization of the Colonial Conferences'.[20] Regarding the composition of the future Conference, which it proposed should better be called 'the Imperial Council', the Lyttelton dispatch said: 'The Secretary of State for the Colonies would represent His Majesty's Government. India, whenever her interests required it, would also be represented. The other members of the Council would be the Prime Ministers of the Colonies represented at the Conference of 1902.'[21]

The meeting of the fourth Colonial Conference, due in 1906, was delayed. In the meantime the Unionists went out of power and were replaced by the Liberals in Britain. The new Parliament contained quite a few members who vigorously championed the cause of India's representation at the forthcoming Conference.[22] One of them, Sir Henry Cotton, an ex-Indian civil servant who had presided over the 1904 session of the Indian National Congress, even suggested in 1906 that the British government should not only invite a representative official of the government of India to attend the Conference, 'but also a representative of the people themselves, chosen, if need be, by the Government from among the non-official members of the Legislative Councils'.[23] The Liberal government favoured the representation of India at the Conference.[24] On 29 May 1906 the prime minister, Sir Henry Campbell-Bannerman, announced in the Commons: 'The practice adopted at the previous Conferences provides for the presence of representatives of different Departments of the Government and under this arrangement the representation of India will be secured.'[25] H.H. Asquith, the chancellor of the exchequer, reiterated the same assurance in Parliament on 19 February 1907. He also declared: 'The question of the representation of India at future Conferences will no doubt enter into the discussion of the future constitution of the Conference itself.'[26] The character and manner of India's proposed representation at the Colonial Conference of 1907 were explained by John Morley, the secretary of state for India, in a letter to Lord Minto, the viceroy: 'About the Colonial Conference which is to assemble by and by, we have promised—as you know—that India should be represented, but of course it cannot be represented in the same sense in which Canada or Australia is. The idea is that the Secretary of State for India should be there, with a sort of assessor, perhaps two: I am thinking of Sir James Mackay and Mr. Holderness.'[27]

The Colonial Conference of 1907 was attended by Morley,[28] Mackay[29] and Holderness.[30] The India Office presented a 'memorandum on preferential tariffs in their relation to India' to the Conference.[31] Mackay also put forward ably the Indian point of view on the subject of preferential trade at the meetings of the Conference.[32] The representatives of the self-governing colonies, particularly those of Australia, jealous of their freedom and status, did not take kindly to India's presence at the Conference table.³³ Their objections appear to have been mainly on three grounds: first, that India was not self-governing,³⁴ secondly, that her representation would only mean an additional vote and influence for Great Britain in the deliberations of the Conference,³⁵ and thirdly, that the paramount consideration of the British government for their Indian trade made them averse to the scheme of preferential tariffs on which the self-governing colonies were very keen.³⁶

At the 1907 Conference the self-governing colonies decided to style themselves 'Dominions'.³⁷ By another resolution it was agreed that future Conferences should be designated 'Imperial' and devoted to the discussion of questions of common interest 'as between His Majesty's Government and his Governments in the self-governing Dominions beyond the seas'.³⁸ The peers of the Empire thus separated themselves from its subject communities. The constitution of the Imperial Conference now became fixed. Self-government was the qualification for its membership and it could only be attended by ministers.³⁹

The published report of the proceedings of the 1907 Conference does not reveal what was actually the decision of the Conference on the subject of India's representation at its future meetings. Ministerial replies to questions in Parliament, however, indicate that, though the Conference was henceforth to be confined to the autonomous governments of the Empire, the secretary of state for India could be present when Indian interests required it.⁴⁰ 'India will be represented at the Imperial Conference by the Secretary of State in all matters in which her interests are or may be involved,' assured the prime minister, Asquith, on 22 March 1911.⁴¹ India, accordingly, made a brief appearance at the Imperial Conference of 1911. The secretary of state for India, Lord Crewe, along with Sir Herbert Risley, an official of his department, was present on the eleventh day of its meeting and addressed the Conference on the need for treating sympathetically the question of Indian immigrants to the dominions.⁴²

India's services to the British Empire in the First World War strengthened her claim for full representation at the Imperial Conference. In July 1915 a non-official member of the Indian legislative council gave notice of a resolution which demanded that in future the government of India should, like those of the dominions, be directly represented at the Imperial Conference.

The viceroy, Lord Hardinge, and his executive council favoured the acceptance of the resolution and wrote to the secretary of state, Austen Chamberlain, to that effect.[43] After consulting the cabinet, Chamberlain authorized the viceroy to accept the resolution, but asked him to make it clear that, while the British government would give a sympathetic consideration to the demand, they could not bind themselves to its principles or details, and that the ultimate decision in the matter would rest with the Imperial Conference itself.[44]

On 22 September 1915, the resolution was formally moved in the Indian legislative council by Sir Muhammad Shafi, who claimed that not merely on the ground of the magnitude of her interests affected should India in justice have a voice in imperial deliberations, the part she had played and was playing in the war showed that she was actually worthy of exercising the privilege for which she asked.[45] The viceroy spoke immediately after the mover and announced that his government gladly accepted the resolution and, if the council passed it, would readily take action upon it. He told the council that he had been 'authorized by His Majesty's Government, while preserving their full liberty of judgment, and without committing them either as to principles, or details, to give an undertaking that an expression of opinion from this Imperial Legislative Council, in the sense of the Resolution that is now before us, will receive most careful consideration on their part, as expressing the legitimate interest of the Legislative Council in an Imperial question, although the ultimate decision of His Majesty's Government must necessarily depend largely on the attitude of other members of the Conference'.[46] Hardinge himself answered some of the possible objections that could be raised against India's membership of the Imperial Conference. Much had happened, he said, since the last Conference was held in 1911 which would leave a lasting mark upon the British Empire and to him it was inconceivable that dominion statesmen would not have realized the great and important position that India occupied within the Empire. 'It is true', Hardinge went on, 'that India is not a self-governing Dominion but that seems hardly a reason why she should not be suitably represented at future Conferences. India's size, population, wealth, military resources, and, lastly, her patriotism demand it.'[47] Hardinge asserted that no Conference could afford to debate great Imperial issues in which

India was vitally concerned, and at the same time to disregard her. How could questions of the defence of the Empire be discussed without India which was 'the greatest military asset of the Empire outside the United Kingdom'; or of commerce without 'England's best customer'? asked Hardinge.[48] He concluded by saying: 'To concede the direct representation of India at future Imperial Conferences does not strike me as a very revolutionary or far-reaching concession to make to Indian public opinion and to India's just claims, and I feel confident that if, and when, this question is placed in its true light before the Governments of the self-governing Dominions, they will regard it from that wider angle of vision from which we hope other Indian questions may be viewed in the near future, so that the people of India may be made to feel what they really are, in the words of Mr Asquith, "conscious members of a living partnership all over the world under the same flag".'[49]

The Indian legislative council passed the resolution unanimously and the government of India's attitude in meeting it more than half-way gladdened the hearts of Indian politicians. The proposal was well received in the United Kingdom and the dominion press. The *Round Table* pleaded for India's representation at the Imperial Conference. It argued that constitutional niceties need not be pressed too far. The Imperial Conference was not a sovereign body. It had no executive authority or legislative power. It was a purely deliberative and consultative piece of machinery which could easily accommodate a representative of a great dependency like India. What India asked for, said the quarterly, might be an anomaly, but mere logic and pedantry should not decide a question which was essentially one of imperial statesmanship. If India was disappointed in the matter, her people would feel it acutely, for with them it was far more a gain of status and recognition that was sought than any material advantage. The *Round Table* also suggested that any existing differences between India and the dominions, such as those concerning Indian immigrants, stood a better chance of being solved by Indian and dominion representatives talking over the matter face to face at the Imperial Conference, more so now because the trenches and the hospitals had afforded to each a wholly new understanding of the other's character.[50]

In a confidential memorandum submitted to the secretary of

state for India in October 1915, Hardinge not only reiterated the arguments he had advanced in favour of India's direct representation at the Imperial Conference in his speech to the Indian legislative council, but even added a few more. He referred, for instance, to the Conference in 1909 on 'the naval and military defence of the Empire' from which India was excluded, 'although it must have been known to all those present that the Empire, as it stands, could not go on without the Indian Army to help it in its defence in many quarters of the globe, and that the annual military expenditure of India was then several times the total military expenditure of all the self-governing Dominions'.[51] 'Although India had no voice in the proceedings of this Conference,' Hardinge added, 'proposals seriously affecting Indian interests, to which public opinion in India would have been strongly opposed, and to which I am convinced, no Government of India could possibly agree, were nevertheless made as a result of the meeting. I refer to the proposal for a larger naval contribution from India.'[52] Hardinge also referred to the statements made in the press that the dominions were to have a voice in the future peace negotiations and remarked that if an Imperial Conference was to be held for this purpose, India's direct representation at it would be 'specially desirable', 'in view of the great Indian interests involved in Persia, Arabia and Mesopotamia, and of the part played by India in the war'.[53] Hardinge argued that India was 'the key-stone of the structure of the British Empire, and ought to be recognized and reckoned with as such'.[54] It would be no more incongruous, he said, to place India alongside the self-governing dominions than it was to classify her with the crown colonies. He suggested that her position 'as that of a great, but not self-governing, dependency' would be sufficiently defined if she were represented at the next Imperial Conference by her secretary of state and one or two official representatives from India as colleagues selected in consultation with the viceroy.[55]

The government of India under Lord Chelmsford—Hardinge's successor to the viceroyalty—continued pleading earnestly with the home government for India's representation at the Imperial Conference. On 16 June 1916 they wrote to the secretary of state for India that 'the interests of India in the Empire, no less than the interests of the Empire in India, fully justify her admission in some definite form to the deliberations of an imperial council'.[56]

Again on 24 November 1916, the government of India pleaded with the secretary of state that India's claim for representation should not be prejudiced by the fact that she was not, and could not for a long time become, a fully self-governing nation. 'That very fact', they argued, 'indeed constitutes the strongest possible reason why her interests and claims should receive the most impartial and punctulious attention at the hands of the conference. Her vast territory, her huge population, her undeveloped resources, her great potential wealth when once those resources are prudently developed, and last, but not least, her loyal support to the Empire during the present crisis, plead most eloquently on her behalf. It would ill become a great Empire, as it reckons up the sum total of its own assets, to dwell with pardonable pride on that territory, that population, those resources, and that loyal support of India, and then to turn a cold shoulder to her just petition.'[57]

The government of India were preaching to the converted. The British government had already decided in favour of admitting India to the Imperial Conference.[58] It was the self-governing dominions which had really to be persuaded to accept India's being placed, as Lord Curzon once remarked, 'at the "high table" in the banquet hall of the Empire States'.[59] Austen Chamberlain had informed Hardinge privately in August 1915: 'I fear we must anticipate great difficulties with [the] self-governing Dominions.'[60] The India Office had to work hard in order to overcome these difficulties. It seized every available opportunity to plead India's case before the dominions and to mollify their objections to India's full representation at the Imperial Conference. One such instance of special pleading on behalf of India deserves mention. Speaking before a conference of the Empire Parliamentary Association in London in the summer of 1916, Lord Islington, the under-secretary of state for India, strongly recommended India's inclusion into the inner circle of the Empire because of 'her size, her geographical position, volume of trade, intellectual and political development, and . . . her proved loyalty to the Crown'.[61] He earnestly appealed to the delegates from the various parliaments of the dominions present on the occasion to 'act as influential missionaries' to their respective parliaments 'to induce them to realize what India is, what its position is, what its value is, within the Empire—the part that it is playing and will continue increasingly to play in the future as a component part of the Empire'.[62] 'How inextricably interwoven are her interests with ours; and ours with hers,'[63] remarked Islington. There was not, he said, a single problem of imperial interest in which India was not directly concerned. And he emphasized repeatedly that no imperial organization could be lasting or effective, complete or adequate to its purpose, which did not include within it a representative of the empire of India.

The dominions were not to be converted so easily. It was not simply a case, as Islington had suggested, of their old ideas about India dying hard. The dominions were extremely jealous of their self-governing status and could not easily allow it to be obscured or compromised by getting mixed up with the less developed parts of the Empire. They might even have suspected a sinister design on the part of Downing Street to bring them down to the level of India. Moreover, the dominions were determined to remain white and they feared that India's elevation to the membership of the Imperial Conference would be the thin end of the coloured wedge.

Whatever the reasons—and here we can only guess—the dominions did not welcome the idea of admitting India to the Imperial Conference when it was first mooted to them officially in September 1916. The prime ministers of Australia and Canada —William Hughes and Robert Borden—expressed themselves definitely adverse; those of New Zealand and South Africa— William Massey and General Botha—remained non-committal.[64] But the secretary of state for India, Austen Chamberlain, was insistent on India's inclusion and he had behind him the support of the government and the people of India. He argued that it would be 'little short of an outrage', in view of India's enormous sacrifices in the war and the hopes aroused in that country by the utterances of British statesmen themselves, to deny her a place in the Imperial Conference. The primary concern of the forthcoming Conference, he added, would be to concert measures in the further prosecution of the war and to this end consultation with the government of India, who had been bearing such a large part of the burden, was absolutely essential.[65] The prime minister, Lloyd George, supported Austen Chamberlain and the War Cabinet decided unanimously in favour of India's inclusion.[66] In order to overcome the difficulty created by the lack of understanding with the dominions, it was agreed to give the Conference a different designation and summon it 'on a special basis, outside the official constitution'.[67]

On 25 December 1916, when Lloyd George summoned the Imperial War Conference, the secretary of state for India was invited to represent India. Austen Chamberlain telegraphed to the viceroy, Chelmsford, to select two gentlemen from India to assist him at the proposed gathering.[68] It was later decided to invite a representative of the Indian princely states as well. The Imperial War Conference and the Imperial War Cabinet commenced their sittings in London in March 1917. India was represented on both bodies by her secretary of state, aided by three delegates from India, Sir James Meston, Sir Satyendra Prasanna Sinha and the Maharaja of Bikaner. The Indian delegates were warmly welcomed and they created a good impression both inside the Conference and outside. Austen Chamberlain immediately took advantage of this fact and with 'the active good will' of the secretary of state for the colonies, Walter Long, pushed forward the claim of India for full representation at the regular Imperial Conference.[69] On 4 April 1917 the Imperial War Conference decided to pass a resolution recommending a modification of the constitution of the regular Imperial Conference so as to permit of India's participation at its future meetings.[70] A formal resolution to this effect was duly passed on 13 April.[71] On Sinha's suggestion, which was readily accepted, India also found a mention in the famous constitutional resolution moved by Sir Robert Borden on 16 April 1917, which claimed for the dominions and India a 'right to an adequate voice in foreign policy and in foreign relations'. But while the dominions were described in this resolution as 'autonomous nations of an Imperial Commonwealth', India could only be called 'an important portion of the same'.[72]

The Indian delegates not only participated in the proceedings of the Imperial War Conference, they 'attended...every meeting of the Imperial War Cabinet, sat on its Committees, and saw every confidential paper, and heard every confidential statement that was made in the course of the sittings of that body'.[73] How real and far-reaching was the progress made in 1917 in respect of India's position in the Empire can be gleaned from a letter of the secretary of state to the viceroy, dated 15 May 1917, communicating to the latter the decisions of the Imperial War Cabinet as regards its future meetings. 'An Imperial Cabinet', Austen Chamberlain informed Chelmsford, 'is to meet once a year. This Cabinet will comprise those British Ministers specially concerned with Imperial questions, including the Secretaries of State for India and the Colonies. There will also be convoked the Prime Ministers of the self-governing Dominions and a representative of the Government of India who will come on the same footing as they do, and is the nearest approximation which India can produce under present circumstances to a Prime Minister. We have further secured that in all future Imperial Conferences India will be represented on a footing of perfect equality with the self-governing Dominions.'[74]

'The admission of India to the Conference,' says Professor Keith Hancock, 'which should normally have been the sequel to Indian self-government, was a recognition of the fact that self-government was India's destiny. It was, so to speak, a payment in advance which India had earned by her extraordinary services.'[75] This was confirmed four months later, on 20 August 1917, when the British government explicitly committed themselves to the policy of 'the progressive realisation of responsible government in India as an integral part of the British Empire'.[76] Significantly enough, this policy was agreed upon not only by the British Cabinet but by the Imperial War Cabinet as a whole.[77] Having admitted India to partnership on equal terms, the imperial statesmen might well have told themselves, 'Let us at least educate our partner'. The resolution passed by the Imperial War Conference on 13 April 1917 was, wrote Lloyd George later, 'important, not merely because it opened the door for the future appearance of India alongside the Dominions at Imperial Conferences, but because it marked the first Imperial recognition of the altered status of India. It was one of the preliminary stages of the reforms on Indian administration, which started that great country on the pathway towards full self-government within the British Commonwealth'.[78] It also led, one might add, to India's participation in the Peace Conference at Paris in 1919 and to her membership, as the only non-self-governing country, of the League of Nations. Far more momentous, however, were the consequences of the decision of 1917 in the realm of Commonwealth development in general. It almost predetermined India's continued membership of the Commonwealth after she became independent in 1947.[79]

6

THE MONTAGU DECLARATION OF 1917*

British policy in India, though liberal and progressive on the whole, lacked until 1917 a sense of direction. Conditions which had made the establishment and continuance of British rule possible in India were fast changing—mainly as a result of that rule itself. There was, however, little conscious effort to direct these changes to a definite and preconceived goal. Concessions were made to the demands of Indian nationalists, but no attempt was made to think out and work out a policy of continuous advance. The reforms of 1892 and 1909 did not shift the foundations of British rule; they merely adjusted the machinery of British government to the changed circumstances in India. They aimed at associating Indians more closely with the administration and allowing them better opportunities of influencing it, while retaining intact its foreign and autocratic character.

The purpose of this paper is to describe how the need for a well-defined and forward-looking British policy *vis-a-vis* the growing nationalist feeling in India came to be increasingly felt and how in August 1917 the British government committed themselves explicity to the policy of preparing India for responsible government within the Empire.

*On 20 August 1917, Edwin Samuel Montagu, the secretary of state for India, declared in the House of Commons: 'The policy of His Majesty's Government, with which the Government of India are in complete accord, is that of the increasing association of Indians in every branch of the administration, and the gradual development of self-governing institutions, with a view to the progressive realisation of responsible government in India as an integral part of the British Empire.' 87 H.C. Deb. 5s., col. 1695.

With the impressions of the Calcutta session of the Indian National Congress fresh in his mind, Samuel Smith wrote to John Morley, the secretary of state for India, on 26 December 1906, about the demand for Indian self-government put forward by Dababhai Naoroji in his presidential address: 'I felt the force of the appeal. No one with a sense of humanity could but feel the great wave of emotion which is carrying India towards an unknown future. It was an epoch-making occasion ... the demand was explicit, and momentous consequences will hang on the answer that we give.'[1] Morley had already given his answer to G.K. Gokhale in the summer of 1906. He had privately assured the leader of the moderate Indian nationalists that he and the viceroy, Lord Minto, were eager to make an effective move in the direction of 'reasonable reforms'. But he was frankly sceptical about Gokhale's 'ultimate hope and design—India to be on the footing of a self-governing colony'. 'For many a long day to come', he had told Gokhale, '—long beyond the short span of time that may be left to us—this was a mere dream.'[2] It was Morley's considered belief that parliamentary democracy was not suited to Indian conditions. He repeatedly denounced in public the idea of introducing it in India as 'a fantastic and ludicrous dream'[3] and a 'gross and dangerous sophism'.[4] He spiritedly repudiated the suggestion that his reforms could in any way lead to a parliamentary system in India.[5]

India was too vast and too divided. She was educationally and economically backward. One can, therefore, understand why the disciple of John Stuart Mill did not 'think it desirable or possible or even conceivable, to adapt English political institutions to the nations who inhabit India'.[6] But what one cannot understand or excuse is the fact that Morley did not suggest an alternative method of India's political evolution. This omission was all the more reprehensible on the part of a statesman who realized that the British Raj was 'intensely artificial and unnatural' and surely could not last.[7] The reforms which he, in collaboration with Minto, introduced into the government of India in 1909 were a typical product of that nineteenth-century English liberalism which believed that statesmanship was mainly a question of determining how far popular demands should be conceded, but which seldom bothered to think out the fundamentals of policy or relate it to a well-defined larger purpose. 'Lacking a clearly distinguishable and steadily developing British policy towards the growth of politics in India,' justly comments Professor C. H. Philips, 'Morley and Minto were driven to devising not so much a coherent plan as a series of expedients to meet the particular and admittedly difficult situation.'[8] A few Indians were admitted to the *arcana imperii*.[9] The numbers and powers of the existing legislative councils were increased.[10] The avowed purpose of these changes, however, was not to train Indians in self-government, but simply 'to enable Government the better to realize the wants, the sentiments, of the governed, and on the other hand, to give the governed a better chance of understanding as occasion arises, the case for the Government against the misrepresentations of ignorance and malice'.[11] In a sense, Morley and Minto refused to face the basic question posed by Indian nationalism: what is the goal of British rule in India? They really gave no serious thought to the future. Morley believed in leaving the day after tomorrow to Providence,[12] and Minto thought he could not afford 'to speculate on the problems of coming generations'.[13] Nor is there anything to show that they ever considered what would be the next step to be taken from the point reached in 1909. 'But what will the next great change be, and when?' asked Minto, only to add 'Not in our time'.[12] For the tired and ageing Morley one step was enough. And he hoped that Indians, too, in so far as they were wise, would not concern themselves with the distant scene. Speaking on the second reading of the Indian Councils Bill in the House of Lords on 23 February 1909, Morley remarked that the effect of his reforms had been, was being and would be to persuade those who hoped for 'autonomy or self-government of the colonial species or pattern' in India to give up their dream and be content with admission to co-operation with the British administration.[15]

This was mere wishful thinking. Men do not give up their dreams so easily: and national dreams are, perhaps, the most tenacious. The eyes of most educated Indians were now fixed on the future and, despite the assertions of Morley and Minto to the contrary, they had welcomed the reforms of 1909 as an advance towards parliamentary self-government. As was to be expected, Indian nationalists, instead of relinquishing their dream, began persuading the British government to accept it as their own. In July 1911 Gokhale wrote that the political evolution to which

Indian reformers looked forward was 'representative government on a democratic basis'. In his view 'the first requisite of improved relations on an enduring basis between Englishmen and Indians' was 'an unequivocal declaration on England's part of her resolve to help forward the growth of representative institutions in India and a determination to stand by this policy, in spite of all temptations or difficulties'. 'I think the time has come', Gokhale added, 'when a definite pronouncement on this subject should be made by the highest authority entitled to speak in the name of England, and the British Government in India should keep such pronouncement in view in all its actions.'[16]

Nor did Indian nationalists stand alone in demanding a definition of British policy in India. Indian unrest and the controversial character of the Morley-Minto reforms had set reflecting Englishmen thinking about the future and purpose of the Raj. Men of religion were, perhaps, the first to respond to the challenge of Indian nationalism. The Bishop of Southampton, for example, enquired in January 1908 whether the English administrators in India ever cared to think where their work in India was leading to. 'Is India', he asked, 'always to remain a subject country? Is that our intention? Is that our desire and inward purpose? Is that our conception of our mission, or have we in our minds something better and nobler, something of more world-wide importance? Have we visions of an Indian nation as a far-off possibility, and are such visions the inspiration of our work? Do we feel that our duty to India and mankind can only be accomplished through the evolution of a united, free, intelligent, self-governing people, and that it cannot be accomplished through the indefinite continuance of foreign bureaucratic rule, however good and beneficent?' The Bishop argued that Englishmen and Indians were working at cross purposes because they did not have the same aim. He pleaded for a meeting of minds on the subject of the future goal and a definite acceptance by the British people of the Indian ideal of self-government.[17]

The enlightened English administrator in India also felt the need of a definite, far-sighted policy. Lovat Fraser noted in 1909: 'Many of our difficulties are due to the fact that we have never made up our minds as to our purpose there.... Reflecting civil servants have said to me: "What are we here for? If I only knew that, I should know how to order my life and my duty." The civilian nowadays is perplexed and puzzled. He sees the conflict of rival ideas—the one that we are in India for the good of the people, and the other that we are there for our own good.'[18] In the same year William Marris was telling Lionel Curtis that 'self-government ... however far distant, was the only intelligible goal of British policy in India. It needed a guiding principle and no other was thinkable.'[19] In June 1912 another distinguished member of the Indian Civil Service, Sir James Meston, was arguing with his friends of the Round Table group in England: 'Do we intend to give her [India] self-government or to hold her permanently in the status of a subject country? Many people would reply that our duty to India is fulfilled when we give her peace and ensure the maintenance of law and order. I do not agree with this narrow conception of our duty. It seems to me that we owe to India an endeavour to raise her by degrees as near to our own plane of civilization as we can. If this be true, self-government, being one of the characteristics of our civilization, must become one of the ideals at which our rule in India is to aim.'[20] Meston disclosed later that the far-reaching and constantly spreading spirit of nationalism in India made it impossible for the British officials in that country to carry on without a declared policy of what England meant to do in India and with India, and that it was largely in response to their appeals that the search for a policy was undertaken.[21]

The radicals in England demanded that the issue should be burked no longer. In July 1910 Josiah Wedgwood asked bluntly in the Commons: 'Do we actually want India some time to be free and self-governing or do we not?' If not, the British government should, he argued, drop cant and say so. If, on the other hand, they did want India to be ultimately self-governing—'whether it be in twenty or fifty or a hundred years'—they should tell that frankly to the Indian people and lay their plans accordingly.[22]

In 1911-12 there was an episode which, though it brought forth renewed and more emphatic official disclaimers of the ideal of dominion self-government for India, revealed that even the government of India felt the need for looking ahead and at least one member of His Majesty's government realized that a clear and authoritative enunciation of British policy in India was imperative. In a dispatch to the secretary of state, dated 25 August 1911, the government of India had pointed out that 'in the course of time, the just demands of Indians for a larger share in the Government of the country will have to be satisfied, and the question will be how this devolution of power can be conceded without impairing the supreme authority of the Governor-General in Council'. To the government of India 'the only possible solution of the difficulty' appeared to be 'gradually to give the Provinces a larger measure of self-government, until at last India would consist of a number of administrations, autonomous in all provincial affairs, with the Government of India above them all and possessing power to interfere in cases of misgovernment, but ordinarily restricting their functions to matters of Imperial concern'.[23] The dispatch was published on 12 December 1911, and was at once seized upon by Indian nationalists as indicating the aim and intention of the British government in India. Speaking at Cambridge on 28 February 1912, Edwin Samuel Montagu, the under-secretary of state for India, confirmed the Indian interpretation of the dispatch. He dwelt at length on the Liberal ideal of the Empire, based on freedom and free association. He remarked that Curzon as viceroy was a mere administrator who had no policy at all. He compared him to a chauffeur who spent his time polishing up the machinery, screwing every nut and bolt of his car ready to make it go, but never driving it or knowing where to drive it to. Referring to the celebrated passage in the government of India dispatch, Montagu remarked: 'That statement shows the goal, the aim towards which we propose to work—not immediately, not in a hurry, but gradually.' He pointed out that the British government could not 'drift on for ever without stating a policy'. A new generation had grown up in India which asked 'What are you going to do with us?'; the extremists had drawn up and published their own exposition of the exact form of *swaraj* which they wanted; the moderates looked to the authorities to say what lines their future policy was to take. 'We have never answered that,' Montagu added, 'and we have put off answering them far too long. At last, and not too soon, a Viceroy has had the courage to state the trend of British policy in India and the lines upon which we propose to advance.'[24]

A storm of controversy raged for a few months in England over the passage in the government of India's dispatch. The Opposition in Parliament accused the Liberal government of contemplating the introduction of some sort of federal home rule in

India. The secretary of state for India, Lord Crewe, repeatedly denied the charge. He explained away the controversial passage in the dispatch as a casual remark, indicating 'the inevitable trend and tendency of things in India' towards further decentralization in all matters of a provincial nature.[25] He referred to the political school in India which cherished the dream of self-government on the dominion model and remarked: 'I say quite frankly that I see no future for India on those lines. I do not believe that the experiment...of attempting to confer a measure of self-government, with practical freedom from Parliamentary control, upon a race which is not our own...is one which could be tried.'[26] Crewe affirmed that there were three objects of British policy in India: 'to devolve upon local and provincial governments as many of the functions of government as can be safely entrusted to them'; 'to employ as many Indians in the public service as can reasonably be employed'; and 'to continue the pursuit of the two first with the maintenance and permanence of British rule in India'.[27] But though Crewe tried, with all the weight of his great authority as secretary of state, to dismiss the idea of a self-governing Indian dominion as 'a world as remote as any Atlantis or Erewhon that ever was thought of by the ingenious brain of an imaginative writer',[28] the last word in the debate lay with the Liberal peer, Lord Courtney. The latter deprecated the tendency 'to put the limit of impossibility on the development that may occur in India'. He recalled the extraordinary changes going on in the eastern world and the remark made to him by Sir Alfred Lyall shortly before his death, 'It is not impossible that the twentieth century may see the complete withdrawal of Europe from Asia', and observed: 'However comfortable it may be to ourselves to attempt to dismiss these speculations, we cannot get rid of them.'[29]

Crewe's invocation of what William Archer called 'the dogma of perpetuity',[30] failed to silence the heretics in India or in England. In December 1912 the council of the All-India Muslim League adopted as one of its objectives 'the attainment of a system of self-government suitable to India'.[31] Returning from India after a short visit in 1912, Philip Kerr wrote in the September *Round Table* that, whether the pace be fast or slow, the goal towards which events in India, propelled by Indian and British alike, were travelling was self-government like that of the dominions.³² Under a very suggestive title 'India: Old Ways and New', another contributor wrote in the December 1912 issue of the same quarterly that conditions in India were changing with a rapidity unknown to previous generations, which made it impossible for the English in that country to go on doing their work empirically, avoiding a philosophy or a creed. And he added: 'It is time we defined our ideas; that we knew clearly what it is that India wants, and how far and by what stages we are going to assist her to get it.'³³

With all their habitual disinclination to speculate about the future, with all their distaste for the conscious and the explicit, the British could not for long avoid defining their policy in India. The need for such a definition was being felt by many. It was, in a fundamental sense, made inevitable by the challenge of Indian nationalism. The impact of the First World War only brought the issue to a head and allowed it to be treated from a new angle of vision. The reforms of 1909, which Morley had hoped would suffice for a generation, had revealed their inadequacy even by 1912-13.³⁴ They had carried the representation of Indians on the legislative councils up to a point at which the question of responsible government in India was bound to arise. Their extension could not be undertaken—as was realized in 1916-17—without first answering the pregnant question 'Whither?'.

India's splendid rally to the cause of the British Empire in the First World War both surprised and gratified the British people who had been hearing so much and so often of Indian unrest in the preceding years. And the more they were surprised and gratified, the more fulsome and vocal were their admiration and gratitude. It was recognized on all hands that India had qualified for closer partnership and a further instalment of reforms. The revelation that India had proved to be not a cause of anxiety but a source of immense strength in the Empire's hour of peril converted even the most conservative imperialist in Britain to view the problems of her internal development and place in the Empire from a changed angle. Even in the past it had been morally impossible for most Englishmen to reject outright the Indian claim for self-government. In view, however, of India's comradeship in the war and Britain's declared war aims, the Indian claim became irresistible. Wherever the question was debated—in the Round Table group, in the viceroy's executive council, or in the War Cabinet—there seemed to be but one answer, consistent with logic, history and tradition: self-government was the only conceivable goal of British rule in India; and the Indian demand for it was a sign of grace and not an evidence of original sin.

Like most of his countrymen, Lord Willingdon, the governor of Bombay, had been profoundly impressed by India's loyal and magnificent services in the war and felt that she should be rewarded handsomely. Early in 1915 he asked Gokhale privately to submit to him a scheme of minimum reforms which would satisfy India after the war, Gokhale submitted his suggestions on 17 February 1915.[35] Tragically, two days later he died. Willingdon wrote to leaders at home to make a reassuring move, but 'either got no answer or no encouragement'.[36] Pherozeshah Mehta soon followed Gokhale to the grave, and the Congress was thus robbed of the moderating influence of two of its most prominent leaders. Under the influence of the excitement of the times, the uncertainty as to the intentions of the government, and the apprehensions regarding India's position in a probable federation of the Empire, the political cauldron in India began to boil. Mrs Annie Besant acted as the peacemaker between Moderates and Extremists and began preparations for launching a home rule movement. The followers of Gokhale and Mehta were anxious that nothing should be done which might embarrass the authorities in any way during the period of the war, but neither did they wish to allow India's case to go by default. The loyalty of Moderates was as firm as their patriotism. They stood for a gradual and peaceful advance of India towards self-government, in co-operation with their British rulers. For themselves they believed 'with the fervour of a religious faith'[37] that India would some day achieve her self-government within the Empire and that British statesmen would prove true to their traditional genius and recognize India's aspirations as legitimate and worthy of encouragement. But how could they—without appearing ridiculous—avow their faith openly while the solemn disclaimers of Morley and Crewe were fresh in public memory? These disclaimers, Moderates knew, had made large classes of people in India distrustful of British good intentions and hostile to British rule. Clearly there was need that these unfortunate disclaimers themselves should first be disclaimed. And this, Moderates felt, could easily be done if the British government made an authoritative and unequivocal declaration that it was their aim and intention to grant India self-government similar to that enjoyed by the dominions in the fullness of time. There was yet another reason why Moderates considered such a declaration of British policy in India necessary. They were wise and practical-minded enough to realize that the war had given rise to excessive hopes and demands in India which no reforms granted by the authorities at the end of the war would suffice to satisfy. Dissatisfaction with post-war reforms might even lead to a recrudescence of serious unrest in the country. But if the government could be persuaded to avow an intention of leading India to self-government, the differences between the rulers and the ruled would be narrowed down to questions of method and pace of advance. In such a situation it would not be difficult for moderate and reasonable men to throw the weight of their influence and co-operation on the side of the authorities, thus ensuring the peaceful but steady political progress of India.

The desire of Moderates for a definite statement that ultimate self-government for India was the goal of British policy found earnest expression in the presidential address delivered by Sir Satyendra Prasanna Sinha to the 1915 session of the Congress held at Bombay. Sinha remarked on the occasion that nothing but 'a rational and inspiring ideal' could 'still the throbbing pain in the soul of awakening India'. After reiterating that self-government within the Empire was the goal of Indian nationalism, he went on to appeal to the British people 'to declare their ungrudging approval of the goal' to which Indians aspired, 'to declare their inflexible resolution to equip India for her journey to that goal and furnish her escort on the long and weary road'. Such a declaration by Britain, Sinha said, would be the most distinguished way of marking her appreciation of India's loyalty and services; it would touch the heart and appeal to the imagination of Indians far more than any specific political reforms. These latter, he argued, might fall short of the high expectations raised by the utterances of English statesmen as to the future place of India in the Empire and cause general disappointment, but an authoritative declaration of Britain's resolve to lead India to self-government would, without causing such disappointment, convince the Indian people that the pace of reforms would be reasonably accelerated and that henceforth it would be only a question of patient preparation. Sinha referred to the 'unhappy statements and even actions of responsible [British] statesmen' in the recent past which had, he said, aroused widespread suspicion in India that Britain did not contemplate giving India freedom even in the most distant future. He demanded, therefore, 'an authentic and definite proclamation with regard to which there will be no evasion, no misunderstanding possible'—'a frank and full statement of the policy of the Government as regards the future of India'—'so that hope may come where despair holds sway and faith where doubt spreads its darkening shadow'. And he warned that unless the British government, 'steadily, consistently and unflinchingly' adhered to the policy of preparing India for ultimate self-government within the Empire 'the moderate party amongst us will soon be depleted of all that is fine and noble in human character'.[38]

That was how Sinha—one of the most loyal and moderate and sensible of Indians—tried to pin down the British nation and government, and tempt them into making a declaration of policy. Lord Chelmsford revealed later that 'the ball was set rolling' by Sinha's remarkable address to the Congress in December 1915.[39] It apparently inspired him—the future viceroy of India—and many others to think about the goal of British policy in India and to realize the need for its announcement.

The ruling viceroy, Lord Hardinge, was a wise and imaginative statesman, fully alive and sympathetic to the new developments in India. Convinced that peace and tranquillity in India and the future good relations between India and the British Empire would depend to a large extent upon what concessions were made to legitimate Indian aspirations, he had already in August 1915 drawn up a memorandum on the reforms which he thought should be introduced in India at the end of the war.[40] In October 1915 he had sent his memorandum to the secretary of state, along with the overwhelmingly favourable comments on it of the heads of local governments and the members of his executive council. Hardinge openly avowed his friendliness to the Indian ideal of self-government. Speaking at the United Services Club at Simla on 8 October 1915, he remarked that it was 'not enough for [England] now to consider only the material outlook of India', she must cherish the aspirations for liberty of which she had herself sown the seed in the country. He asked the English officials in India to prepare themselves for the 'far more glorious task' of the future, that of 'encouraging and guiding the political self-development of the people', and he himself looked forward 'with confidence to a time when ... India may be regarded as a true friend of the Empire and not merely as a trusty dependent'.[41] Although in his valedictory address to the imperial legislative council on 24 March 1916, Hardinge discouraged 'extravagant hopes ... and unrealisable demands' with regard to post-war reforms in India, he did not fail to add: 'I do not for a moment wish to discountenance self-government as a national ideal. It is a perfectly legitimate aspiration and has the warm sympathy of all moderate men.'[42] Hardinge's remarks encouraged Indian politicians to think that it would not be very difficult to persuade the authorities to make a formal and definite declaration that self-government for India was the ultimate goal of their policy.

A powerful combination of intellectuals and politicians in England, known as the Round Table group,[43] was at this time busy exploring the possibilities of imperial federation. During the autumn of 1915, while the group was engaged in examining the position of India *vis-a-vis* a future federated Empire, it met regularly once a fortnight in London. Among those who attended these meetings were Lionel Curtis, Philip Kerr, Reginald Coupland, Sir William Duke, Sir Lionel Abrahams, M.C. Seton, C.H. Kisch, and J.E. Shuckburgh. The group began by agreeing that the attitude taken by the Indians in the war had proved that the country was riper than had been supposed for further reforms. Curtis, however, insisted that it was imperative to decide what was the goal of British policy in India before discussing any further steps in constitutional advance. The only conceivable goal, it was recognized, was self-government. A closer examination of the term 'self-government' revealed that it was ambiguous. 'The only meaning of self-government as a goal which bore the test of examination was responsible government for India within the Commonwealth which could not stop short of those by which the Dominions had reached their present position.'[44] It was obvious that India could not advance by one step to full responsible government and that her progress towards it must be by stages. It was also realized that any further progress on the lines of the Morley-Minto reforms would lead to disaster, for a further increase of the non-official element in the legislative councils would give the latter the power of paralysing government at every turn, but not the power and responsibility of conducting government for themselves. The essence of the problem was, therefore, to find a method of introducing true responsible government in a limited and manageable field of administration, which could be contracted or extended in accordance with the practical results attained, without imperilling the structure of government itself. The method by which this gradual and safe advance to responsible government could be made in India was suggested in a memorandum prepared for the group by Sir William Duke.[45] It was later nicknamed 'dyarchy' and became the basis of the Montagu-Chelmsford reforms. Chelmsford had shown interest in the inquiries of the group and at his request the final draft of the Duke memorandum was sent to him in May 1916. The part played by the Round Table group in determining the form of the announcement of 20 August 1917, in securing the representation of India at the Imperial Conference, and in the subsequent stages of the Montagu-Chelmsford reforms, though not always easy to trace with precision, was certainly significant, if not decisive.

Chelmsford came as viceroy to India in April 1916 with his mind made up that a declaration of British policy was necessary.[46] At the very first meeting of his executive council, held in May 1916, he propounded two questions: '(1) What is the goal of British rule in India? and (2) What are the steps on the road to that goal?'[47] The deliberations of the council led to the conclusion that 'the endowment of British India as an integral part of the British Empire with self-government was the goal of British rule' and that an advance towards this goal should be made along three roads, viz. the development of local self-government; the more responsible employment of Indians in the administration; and the expansion of the provincial legislative councils.[48] On 24 November 1916, the government of India sent a dispatch to the secretary of state, containing their final proposals for reform, along with the comments of the local governments on them.[49] The two main features of the government of India dispatch related to the reform of the provincial legislative councils and the declaration of the goal of British rule in India. As regards the provincial legislative councils, the dispatch had recommended that their electorates should be widened, that the number of Indian representatives in them should be increased, and that they should have elected majorities.⁵⁰ In making these recommendations the government of India had followed the lines laid down by the reforms of 1892 and 1909. They had rejected the method of advance—by way of dyarchy—suggested in the Round Table (Duke) memorandum.⁵¹ Not only had they not recommended any immediate enlargement of the constitutional powers of the provincial legislative councils, they had expressly told the secretary of state that they had 'no wish to develop the councils as quasi-parliaments'.⁵²

As regards the declaration of the goal of British rule in India, the government of India had proposed a long and verbose formula: 'The goal to which we look forward is the endowment of British India as an integral part of the Empire, with self-government, but the rate of progress towards that goal must depend upon the improvement and wide diffusion of education, the softening of racial and religious differences, and the acquisition of political experience.

'The form of self-government to which she may eventually attain must be regulated by the special circumstances of India. They differ so widely from those of any other part of the Empire that we cannot altogether look for a model in those forms of self-government which already obtain in the great Dominions. In all parts of the Empire which now enjoy self-government, it has been the result, not of any sudden inspiration of theoretical statesmanship, but of a steady process of practical evolution, substantially facilitated by the possession of a more or less common inheritance of political traditions, social customs and religious beliefs.

'British India has been built up on different lines, and under different conditions, and must work out by the same steady process of evolution a definite constitution of her own. In what form this may eventually be cast it is neither possible nor profitable for us to attempt now to determine, but we contemplate her gradual progress towards a larger and larger measure of control by her own people, the steady and conscious development of which will ultimately result in a form of self-government, differing perhaps in many ways from that enjoyed by the other parts of the Empire, but evolved on lines which have taken into account India's past history, and the special circumstances and traditions of her component peoples, and her political and administrative entities.'⁵³

Unfortunately the government of India could not take the Indian public into their confidence. Indian politicians had expected some announcement of policy in Chelmsford's opening speech to the imperial legislative council in September 1916, but were disappointed. It was already rumoured that the government of India were busy considering a scheme of future reforms, but when Indian members enquired in the council whether it was so, and would the government publish their proposals before final decision was reached, the home member merely replied that the government were 'unable to make any statement in the matter'.[54] Anxious lest their case go by default, nineteen non-official members of the imperial legislative council hurriedly put their heads together and produced a memorandum, containing what they called their 'humble suggestions' regarding post-war reforms in India, and submitted it to the viceroy in September 1916.

Aided by the unnecessary reticence of the authorities, Indian nationalists closed their ranks. Extremists re-entered the Congress and before the year 1916 was out the Muslim League had signed a concordat with its old antagonist. Besides putting forward joint proposals for an early and far-reaching reform in the government of India, the Congress and the League, meeting together at Lucknow in the last week of December 1916, demanded that 'the King-Emperor should be pleased to issue a proclamation that it is the aim and intention of British policy to confer self-government on India at an early date'.[55] It was a definite and direct demand to which some answer would have to be given by the British government. As a matter of mere courtesy the Congress and the League would have to be told whether their request for a statement of policy was to be granted or not. In February 1917 the Maharaja of Bikaner publicly expressed the deep sympathy of the princes for 'the legitimate aspirations of our brother Indians'.[56] Never before had such a unanimity of opinion been witnessed in India on any political issue. Hindus and Muslims; Moderates and Extremists; politicians and princes—all seemed to be united in their desire for self-government for India. This unique phenomenon could not fail to impress the British government. It was not long before liberal non-official Anglo-Indian opinion reinforced the Indian demand for a declaration of British policy. 'We have never met an intelligent man', wrote the *Times of India* on 15 May 1917, 'who doubted the goal of British policy in India; it is clearly and irrevocably, the attainment of full self-government within the Empire.' The paper could 'discern no possible ill, and many positive advantages', in a 'clear and emphatic announcement' of this goal. 'Unless the end is clearly in view', it added, 'there can be no logical or definite purpose behind such constitutional changes as are made or contemplated.'[57] On 21 June 1917, the paper again urged 'the Government of India to place itself at the head of the best national forces in India, to avow boldly and uncompromisingly that the attainment of self-government within the Empire is the goal of its policy in India'.[58] Similar appeals were made by the Bishops of Calcutta[59] and Madras.[60]

An India Office committee, headed by Sir William Duke, examined the government of India dispatch of 24 November 1916, and submitted its report to the secretary of state on 16 March 1917.[61] The committee did not think that the proposals of the government of India with regard to the provincial legislative councils constituted a coherent and well-thought-out plan of reform, or that they embodied sound and constitutional lines of political advance.[62] It pointed out that a mere increase in the number of elected Indian representatives in the councils would effect 'no progress towards self-government', but simply 'perpetuate and aggravate a vicious system which makes it the main function of the Legislative Councils to oppose and criticise the government while remaining completely free from responsibility for the result of their action'.[63] The committee considered it 'hazardous to increase their numbers while withholding responsibility' and suggested that 'training in functions ought to precede any considerable increase of numbers'.[64] Nor did the committee give its support to the enunciation of an ultimate goal for Indian constitutional development, such as formulated by the government of India. 'We doubt the wisdom', said its report, 'of dangling before the Indian politicians a formula of political progress, hedged with restrictions that nullify its meaning, and calculated to embarrass, by the vagueness of its promises, our successors in Indian government. We feel that the situation demands not the visionary prospect of a development beyond the realisation of generations, but a frank and clear statement embodying practical progressive reforms capable of achievement within a definite future that can be foreseen.'[65]

The secretary of state for India, Austen Chamberlain, agreed with the committee's criticism of the government of India scheme and wrote to the viceroy accordingly.⁶⁶ As regards a declaration of British policy in India, however, Chamberlain had begun to realize its necessity,⁶⁷ though he considered the formula proposed by the viceroy to be unnecessarily elaborate and formal. 'I do not dispute your goal,' he wrote to Chelmsford, 'though I dislike the elaboration and the formality of your definition. I should prefer to say in the least formal manner possible and in the shortest words, that our object is to develop free institutions with a view to ultimate Self-Government within the Empire, and I should not attempt to define, at a time so distant from any point at which we could expect this aspiration to be realised the form which such Self-Government must take or the extent to which our aspiration can ultimately be realised.'⁶⁸ Chamberlain was also anxious that any such statement of the goal of British policy in India should be 'accompanied by a very clear declaration that this is a distant goal' and that 'the rate of progress and the times and stages by which it is to be reached must be controlled and decided by His Majesty's Government'.⁶⁹

In the spring of 1917 the Maharaja of Bikaner, Sir James Meston and Sir Satyendra Prasanna Sinha went to England, as delegates from India, to attend the meetings of the Imperial War Conference. They ardently pleaded India's case for ultimate self-government within the Empire from various platforms in that country and created a very favourable impression. Commenting on their speeches—particularly those of Bikaner—*The Times* wrote on 2 May 1917: 'The question is whether the time is not now upon us for something more than pious aspirations about the future of India.... The broad lines of British policy in India are perfectly clear. It looks steadily forward to a gradual increase of the self-governing function, and is only concerned to regulate that increase as good order within and security against aggression from without require. But this policy is too seldom expressed in terms, and we believe that the moment to declare it with authority is now, while the war is still in progress, and not as a reply to agitation when the war is over.'⁷⁰ In private Bikaner, Meston and Sinha pressed the need for an announcement of British policy upon the secretary of state for India and apparently succeeded in converting him to their view.⁷¹

An additional and a very potent argument, if not for making the announcement, at least for launching India as speedily as possible on the road to responsible self-government, was furnished by the decision of the Imperial War Conference in April 1917 to admit India to the full membership of the regular Imperial Conference. Self-government was the prerequisite for membership of the Imperial Conference and if an exception had been made in India's case, a payment in advance, so to speak, made to her, it was only on the understanding that self-government was her destiny.[72]

Willingdon had, as noted above,[73] since long favoured a bold and liberal gesture in India by the British government. He was in close touch with the leaders of moderate India and sympathetic to their aspirations. Moreover, his province—Bombay—was particularly affected by the home rule agitation of Besant and Tilak. In the autumn of 1916 he had strongly advised the government of India and the secretary of state to make an early declaration of their policy in order to strengthen the hands of the moderates, but was told that it would be useless to make a general declaration until the authorities were prepared to state specifically the reforms which they intended to carry out at the earliest.[74] In May 1917 Willingdon renewed his pressure upon the viceroy[75] and with better effect. On 18 May 1917, the latter telegraphed to the secretary of state requesting an immediate announcement of British policy in India. The viceroy pointed out that the political situation in India had materially altered during the past few months as a result of the revolution in Russia, the publication of statements as to the right of the peoples to govern themselves, the reception accorded to the representatives of India at the War Conference in England, and India's admission to the Imperial Conference. The absence of any definite announcement of policy was, he wrote, causing embarrassment to the local governments, alienating the moderates, and leaving the field free to the extremist propaganda. The viceroy realized the difficulties of making a declaration of policy while not yet being in a position to state specifically what their proposals for reform were, but he considered the declaration necessary 'in order to arrest the further defection of moderate opinion'.[76]

On 22 May 1917, Chamberlain invited the attention of the cabinet to the very serious problems with which the government of India were faced and asked for an early decision on the action to be taken. He circulated to his colleagues the reform proposals submitted by the government of India, along with his comments, and his suggestions for making known the policy of the British government.[77] Lloyd George's small War Cabinet was, however, overburdened with work and could not find time early to deal with the Indian issue.[78] And when at last it did take up the question on 29 June, and again on 5 July, valuable time was wasted in a fruitless discussion over and the meaning of the term 'self-government'. Lord Balfour, in particular, objected to the use of the term 'self-government' in any declaration for the reason that in the mouths of Englishmen it had acquired a definite meaning, namely, a parliamentary form of government, and in his view it was unwise to graft parliamentary democracy on India.[79] The result was that when Austen Chamberlain suddenly resigned on 14 July 1917, over the Mesopotamia affair,[80] the cabinet, even after having discussed the question twice, had failed to reach any decision on the form of the announcement or whether it should be made at all.

In India the political situation had meanwhile further deteriorated. The internment of Mrs Besant in June 1917 had led to a countrywide agitation. The publication of the report of the Mesopotamia commission at the end of June, containing severe strictures on the government of India for their lack of judgement and administrative efficiency, had dealt another blow to their prestige. The debate in the Commons on the report turned out to be a censure motion on the government of India. Montagu, in a bitter and impassioned speech, described the government of India as 'too wooden, too iron, too inelastic, too antediluvian', 'illogical and indefensible', and pleaded for a more responsible and democratic administration. He outlined his vision of future India as 'a series of self-governing provinces and principalities, federated by one central government', and remarked: 'But whatever be the object of your rule in India, the universal demand of those Indians whom I have met and corresponded with is that you should state it.' 'The history of this war shows', Montagu went on, 'that you can rely upon the loyalty of the Indian people to the British Empire—if you ever doubted it! If you want to use that loyalty you must take advantage of that love of country which is a religion in India, and you must give them that bigger opportunity of controlling their destinies, not merely by councils which cannot act, but by control, by growing control, of the executive itself.'[81]

Montagu's speech gladdened the hearts of Indian nationalists. He had ever since his days as the under-secretary of state for India (1910-14) been known for his deep sympathy with Indian national aspirations. And when on 18 July 1917—within a week of his performance in the Mesopotamia debate—Montagu was appointed as Chamberlain's successor at the India Office, the event was widely acclaimed in India and gave rise to excessive expectations. Many believed that he had been selected to carry into effect the views expressed in his Mesopotamia speech. Indian politicians now became more active than ever before. The committee of the Indian National Congress and the council of the Muslim League met together at Bombay in the last week of July and reiterated their demand that the imperial government be pledged to the policy of making India a self-governing member of the Empire. They also urged the authorities to adopt the Congress-League scheme of post-war reforms, to publish the official proposals for discussion, and to reverse 'the policy of repression'. In order to secure these objectives they decided to send a deputation to England and even threatened to launch a campaign of passive resistance in India.[82]

Recognizing 'the gravity and urgency of the situation' in India, the viceroy repeatedly impressed upon the home government the view that, whatever be the decision regarding the nature and extent of future reforms, 'it would be fatal to put off any longer an unmistakable declaration in India of our future policy'.[83] Montagu energetically took up the threads where Chamberlain had left them. On 30 July 1917, he circulated a memorandum to the cabinet, drawing their attention to the rapidly deteriorating situation in India and to the increasing insistence of the viceroy and the heads of provincial governments for an immediate announcement of policy.[34] But he could not get the cabinet to find the time to discuss the question soon.[35] On 7 August he was still pleading with the prime minister: 'You can save India. You can set your foot, and force England to set its foot, firmly on a path of progress on democratic lines. . . .'[86]

Montagu was anxious that any declaration of British policy must include the word 'self-government', not only because it was so current in Indian discussion, but also because he feared that its avoidance might cause dissatisfaction in India and thus defeat the very purpose of making the declaration.[87] The formula which he had suggested to the cabinet in his memorandum of 30 July was substantially the same as that proposed earlier by Chamberlain. It read: 'His Majesty's Government and the Government of India have in view the gradual development of free institutions in India with a view to ultimate self-government within the Empire.'[88]

This, however, did not satisfy Lord Curzon, who like most members of the cabinet disliked the phrase 'self-government'.[89] He devoted a good deal of time and thought to the phraseology of the proposed declaration. In order to make it 'rather safer and certainly nearer to [his] own point of view',[90] he redrafted it as follows on the eve of its publication: 'The policy of His Majesty's Government, with which the Government of India are in complete accord, is that of the increasing association of Indians in every branch of the administration, and the gradual development of self-governing institutions, with a view to the progressive realisation of responsible government in India as an integral part of the British Empire.'[91]

It was this formula which the cabinet sanctioned on 14 August 1917, and Montagu repeated in the Commons six days later— on 20 August—in reply to a question from Charles Roberts. Montagu also declared that substantial steps in pursuance of this policy would be taken as soon as possible and that he would be proceeding to India shortly to discuss matters with the government of India and receive representations from Indians. 'I would add', he went on, 'that progress in this policy can only be achieved by successive stages. The British Government and the Government of India on whom the responsibility lies for the welfare and advancement of the Indian peoples, must be the judges of the time and measure of each advance, and they must be guided by the co-operation received from those upon whom new opportunities of service will thus be conferred, and by the extent to which it is found that confidence can be reposed in their sense of responsibility.'[92]

The announcement laid down clearly and definitely the ultimate aim of British rule in India. It recognized India to be potentially a dominion. It committed the British government to the policy of introducing parliamentary self-government in India on the English model. It was not only 'the most momentous utterance ever made in India's chequered history',[93] it was also a landmark in British imperial history, for it marked a definite repudiation of the concept of 'the two empires'[94]—the concept that there could be, under the British flag, one form of constitutional evolution for the west and another for the east, or one for the white races and another for the non-white. The declaration of 20 August 1917, signified the passing away of the Second British Empire and the beginning of what Zimmern called 'the Third British Empire',[95] the transformation, in principle, of the Empire into a Commonwealth of Nations.

7

GANDHI AND THE BRITISH COMMONWEALTH

Gandhi: The Loyalist

Mohandas Karamchand Gandhi learnt his politics in South Africa where he stayed from 1893 to 1914. Like most English-educated Indians of his generation, he was then a loyal and moderate nationalist. He had a romantic veneration for the British constitution, especially because it recognized the principles of individual freedom and racial equality. He was 'a lover' of the British Empire, because he thought it was on the whole doing good to his country. He believed that Indians could rise to their full stature within and with the help of the Empire. He wanted his countrymen to qualify for equal partnership in the Empire by loyal service and sacrifice. He himself served with distinction in the Boer War and the Zulu rebellion on the side of the English. In his book *Hind Swaraj*, published in 1909, Gandhi vigorously supported the ideals and methods of moderate Congressmen in India and denounced those of the extremists. Though extremely critical of many aspects of western civilization, Gandhi genuinely loved the English people and admired the outstanding qualities of their character.

Throughout World War I Gandhi laboured strenuously in the cause of the defence of the Empire. He preached 'absolutely unconditional and wholehearted co-operation with the government on the part of educated India' in the war effort and emphasized what he considered to be the elementary truth that if the Empire perished, with it would perish their cherished political aspirations for their own country.[1] He disappointed Mrs Annie Besant in 1915 when he refused to join her in launching a home rule movement in India. He told her in so many words that he did not share her distrust of the English people and would do nothing which might embarrass them during the war.² He would have liked his countrymen to 'withdraw all the Congress resolutions, and not whisper "Home Rule" or "Responsible Government" during the pendency of the war'.³ The secretary of state, Edwin Montagu, while in India in 1917, noted in his *Diary* after an interview with Gandhi: '[Gandhi] does not understand details of schemes. He wants the millions of India to leap to the assistance of the British throne.'⁴ Busy recruiting soldiers for the war, Gandhi wrote to the viceroy, Lord Chelmsford, in April 1918 that he loved the English nation and wished to evoke in every Indian the loyalty of Englishmen.⁵ To M.A. Jinnah, who was then engaged, along with Mrs Besant and B.G. Tilak, in popularizing the gospel of home rule, he wrote in July 1918: 'Seek ye first the recruiting office and everything will be added unto you.'⁶

In spite of the ill-timed Rowlatt Act and the unfortunate Amritsar massacre, Gandhi pleaded with his people to work the reforms of 1919 in a spirit of genuine co-operation and good will. At the Amritsar session of the Congress held towards the end of December 1919, the latter-day apostle of non-co-operation would not even brook the idea of grudging acceptance or Irish obstructionism which some of the radicals contemplated practising in the councils.

The Loyalist Turns Rebel

It was the events of the next few months which turned the great loyalist and co-operator into a rebel and a non-co-operator. The terms of the Treaty of Sevres with Turkey, published in May 1920, were considered by most Indians—not only by Muslims—as a breach of the earlier solemn pledges given by British statesmen. The report of the Hunter Commission appeared to them as an attempt to whitewash the culprits in the Amritsar massacre. The manner in which General Dyer's action was acclaimed by a strong element in the House of Commons and a majority in the House of Lords, and the immense public subscription raised for him filled Indians with pain and indignation. Gandhi pleaded with the authorities to put themselves morally right, but the latter failed to appreciate the moral aspect of the issues involved until it was too late. Gandhi became convinced that 'the present representatives of the Empire' had become 'dishonest and unscrupulous', that they had no real regard for the wishes of the Indian people and counted the honour of India as of little consequence.'[7] To an enraged and aggrieved people he suggested the way of non-violent non-co-operation to enforce the national will and secure redress of the Khilafat and Panjab wrongs.

Gandhi's movement of non-violent non-co-operation, launched in August 1920, was more in the nature of an appeal to the English conscience. Gandhi knew that the English were, of all people, peculiarly vulnerable to this weapon. 'An Englishman', he told C.F. Andrews, 'never respects you till you stand up to him. Then he begins to like you. He is afraid of nothing physical; but he is mortally afraid of his own conscience, if you ever appeal to it and show him to be in the wrong. He does not like to be rebuked for wrong-doing at first; but he will think over it, and it will get hold of him and hurt him till he does something to put it right.'[8] Gandhi was, in fact, over-sanguine of his success. He expected his *satyagraha* to be a short and swift campaign to which the British would yield. His judgement was basically sound. Had he been a little less honest and scrupulous, or, as some would say, a better politician than he actually was, he would have scored a resounding triumph by the end of December 1921.[9]

Gandhi's movement was not originally directed against the British Empire. He repeatedly claimed during 1920-2 that in showing to the Indian people the way of non-violent non-co-operation in order to ventilate their grievances, he was rendering a greater service to the Empire than any which he did render in the past.

Swaraj within the Empire

In December 1920 the Congress revised its creed and declared its object to be the attainment of *swaraj* by all legitimate and peaceful means. Gandhi was the author of the formula and he explained that the Congress was to strive for achieving self-government within the Empire, if possible, and without, if necessary. Personally he felt confident that *swaraj* within the Empire was possible. 'I have faith enough in the British people', he wrote in 1921, 'to feel that, whilst they will test our determination and strength to the uttermost, they will not carry it to the breaking-point.'[10] He defined *swaraj* as 'full responsible government on

Dominion lines' and 'full Dominion status' for India.[11] On one point, however, Gandhi was insistent: it must be a free and equal partnership and India must have the right to secede. On 6 October 1920 he wrote: 'We must have absolute equality in theory and practice and ability to do away with the British connection.'[12] 'In a free Commonwealth,' he remarked in June 1921, 'every partner has as much right to retire if the rest go wrong, as it is his duty to remain so long as the rest are faithful to certain common principles.'[13]

Dominion Status v. Independence

The slogan of complete independence outside the British Empire was first raised in India by Aurobindo Ghose and B.C. Pal in 1907, during the days of the anti-partition agitation in Bengal. Its effect was electrifying but short-lived. After 1909 the cry of complete independence had almost died down. Aurobindo retired from politics and Pal became a convert to the idea of imperial federation. The Home Rulers never contemplated severance of the British connexion. Even that stormy petrel, Tilak, did not advocate *swaraj* outside the British Empire. The manifesto of his Congress Democratic Party, which Tilak issued in April 1920, read: 'This party believes in the integration or federation of India in the British Commonwealth for the advancement of the cause of humanity and the brotherhood of mankind, but demands autonomy for India and equal status as a sister state with every partner in the British Commonwealth, including Great Britain.'[14] In the latter half of 1920, however, the demand for complete independence outside the British Empire began to gain strength in India. It was encouraged in part by the events which gave birth to the Khilafat and non-co-operation movements. It was inspired by the similar demand being made in Egypt and Ireland at the time. But it was an Englishman, C.F. Andrews, who did the most to popularize it. In a series of articles and pamphlets,[15] Andrews condemned the idea of self-government for India within the Empire as the product of a subservient mind. He equated the British Empire with racial domination and economic exploitation and told Indians not to delude themselves with the vain hope that they would some day achieve an equal and honourable place within it. India, Andrews said, was a mother country herself and not a daughter nation like the dominions. Race, religion, language, history and culture—all separated her from Britain and the dominions; she could never in reality become an integral part of the British Empire, 'which must always remain peculiarly and centrally British'. Self-government for India within the Empire was, Andrews argued, not only impossible but also undesirable. The British connexion would hamper India's natural and healthy growth. It would involve India in Britain's aggressive wars and perpetuate exploitative western economic interests in the country.

The case for India's independence outside the British Empire was never before or in after years presented with such convincing logic and telling eloquence as it was by Andrews in 1920-1. His preaching made a tremendous impression in India, not least on such alert young minds as that of Jawaharlal Nehru.[16] It failed, however, to convince Gandhi, who claimed to know Englishmen better. Gandhi publicly expressed his dissent from the views of his friend. He rebuked Andrews severely for his lack of faith in the British connexion and for putting forward the demand for complete independence outside the Empire which, he said, had done a great deal of mischief in India. When Andrews remarked, 'It would almost seem as if you had more faith in my own countrymen than I have myself', Gandhi replied, 'That may be true.'[17]

Gandhi had a fundamental, moral objection to the demand for independence outside the Empire. He considered such a demand to be unrighteous—indicating a want of faith in God and in human nature. To say that the English would never grant equal partnership to Indians was, he argued, to suggest that the former were incapable of realizing the first principle of religion, namely, the brotherhood of man. Non-violent non-co-operation, Gandhi never ceased to reiterate, was not a programme for the seizure of power, but for the conversion of Englishmen. The English would be converted when Indians developed internal strength. If they remained unconverted it was the failure of Indians, not of the English. In Gandhi's view it was 'petulant', 'vindictive', and 'religiously unlawful' to refuse an equal and honourable partnership with Britain.[18] 'India's greatest glory', he told his countrymen, 'will consist not in regarding Englishmen as her implacable enemies, fit only to be turned out of India at the first available opportunity, but in turning them into friends and partners in a commonwealth of nations in place of an empire based upon exploitation of the weaker or undeveloped nations and races of the earth and therefore finally upon force.'[19]

It was with such arguments that Gandhi tried to shame into silence the radical idealists in India. There can be little doubt that but for Gandhi's determined opposition the Congress—and even the Muslim League—would have gone over to secession and republicanism in 1920-1. When he was in prison (from March 1922 to February 1924) his arguments were used effectively by the moderate and sober leaders of the nationalists to defy the attempts of the 'Young Turks' to get the Congress committed to the ideal of complete independence, implying severance of the British connexion.

In his presidential address to the Belgaum Congress in December 1924, Gandhi clearly defined his attitude. 'The better mind of the world desires to-day', he remarked, 'not absolutely independent states warring against one another, but a federation of friendly interdependent states. The consummation of that event may be far off. I want to make no grand claim for our country. But I see nothing grand or impossible about our expressing our readiness for universal interdependence. It should rest with Britain to say that she will have no real alliance with India. I desire the ability to be totally independent without asserting the independence. Any scheme that I would frame, while Britain declares her goal about India to be complete equality within the Empire would be that of alliance and not of independence without alliance.'[20] Gandhi urged Congressmen not to insist on independence in each and every case, not because there was anything impossible about it, but because it was wholly unnecessary. 'If the British Government', he argued, 'mean what they say and honestly help us to equality, it would be a greater triumph than a complete severance of the British connection.'[21]

The Balfour Committee Report and General Hertzog's satisfaction with the results of the Imperial Conference of 1926 added strength to Gandhi's elbow. He used it effectively against the separatists when they moved their annual resolution at the 1926 session of the Congress at Gauhati. He told them that between Britain and the dominions there was a partnership at will on terms of equality and that *swaraj* under dominion status implied the right to secede. 'Take the instance', he remarked, 'of South Africa. There is that haughty nation, the Dutch Boers. Even they do not bring in such a resolution. General Hertzog has returned from London completely converted, knowing that it he wants to declare independence today, he can get it. I shall not be satisfied with any constitution that we may get from the British Parliament unless it leaves that power with us also, so that if we choose to declare our independence we could do so.'[22]

Partnership with Great Britain

While Gandhi was busy trying to keep his unruly followers in check, Lord Birkenhead offered the latter a real boon in the form of the Simon Commission of 1927. Amidst the atmosphere of universal indignation aroused in India by the appointment of an exclusively British commission, the radical idealists, led by Jawaharlal Nehru, found it easy to make the Congress pass a resolution in December 1927 declaring 'the goal of the Indian people to be complete national independence'. The creed of the Congress, as defined by the constitution of 1920, remained unchanged, but the separatists had now unfurled their banner. Gandhi was very angry. He denounced the resolution as 'ill-conceived'.[23] 'My ambition', he wrote, 'is much higher than independence. Through the deliverance of India, I seek to deliver the so-called weaker races of the earth from the crushing heels of Western exploitation in which England is the greatest partner. If India converts, as it can, Englishmen, it can become the predominant partner in a world commonwealth of which England can have the privilege of becoming a partner if she chooses.... This is big talk I know. For a fallen India to aspire to move the world and protect weaker races is seemingly an impertinence. But in explaining my strong opposition to this cry for independence, I can no longer hide the light under a bushel. Mine is an ambition worth living for and worth dying for. In no case do I want to reconcile myself to a state lower than the best for fear of consequences. It is, therefore, not out of expediency that I oppose independence as my goal.'[24]

Though Gandhi was able to persuade the Congress in December 1928 to accept the ideal of dominion status postulated in the All-Parties Conference Report, it was with great difficulty and only on the condition that if the government did not accept the report within a year the Congress would inscribe the ideal of complete independence on its banner. This condition not being fulfilled, despite Lord Irwin's well-meant efforts, the Congress decided at Lahore in December 1929 to declare complete independence as its goal. The clever Mahatma, however, once again confounded the radicals. The latter were to have nothing but their pound of flesh. Gandhi judged correctly that a refusal to accept the ideal of complete independence would split the Congress over an unreal issue. He himself fully appreciated the nature of dominion status and the degree of freedom it implied, but he had to make allowance for the sentiments, the prejudices, and what he called 'the inferiority complex' of those who objected to it as an ideal. He therefore decided to satisfy their clamour for complete independence but saw to it that the Congress was not committed to secession. By a formal resolution it was declared that the word *swaraj* in the Congress constitution shall mean complete independence.[25] What this complete independence signified was not defined. In fact, an attempt to do so was foiled by Gandhi. When Subhas Chandra Bose moved an amendment proposing, among other things, the addition of a rider to complete independence 'implying thereby complete severance of the British connection'.[26] Gandhi vigorously opposed it and the Congress agreeing with him rejected it with an overwhelming majority. Even at that Congress session, Gandhi made it clear that the resolution was not a declaration of independence, nor did it preclude association with Britain on terms of equality. Soon after the Congress session he assured the British that the resolution on complete independence need cause no alarm, 'for has it not been admitted by responsible British statesmen that Dominion status is virtual independence?'[27] In fact, he requested the viceroy, Lord Irwin, not to play the game of the extremists in India by branding the demand for complete independence as seditious while extolling the glories of dominion status. Irwin wrote to King George on 13 March 1931 that it was 'definitely untrue to suggest, as I see it suggested that he [Gandhi] is out to break the unity of Your Majesty's Empire'.[28] Irwin conveyed to King George what Gandhi had told him, that in his view 'the highest form' of complete independence for India was one that could be attained 'in association with Great Britain'.[29]

At the second Round Table Conference, which he attended, Gandhi made it clear beyond a shadow of doubt that he did 'not wish to sever the bond, but to transform it', and that what the

Congress demanded was not secession but merely the right to secede. 'If we are intent upon complete independence,' he remarked, 'it is not from any sense of arrogance; it is not because we want to parade before the universe that we have now severed connection with the British people. Nothing of the kind. On the contrary, you will find . . . that the Congress contemplates a partnership—the Congress contemplates a connection with the British people—but that connection to be such as can exist between two absolute equals.'[30] 'Time was,' he added, 'when I prided myself on being, and being called, a British subject. I have ceased for many years to call myself a British subject; I would far rather be called a rebel than a subject. But I have aspired—I still aspire—to be a citizen, not in the Empire, but in a Commonwealth; in a partnership if possible—if God wills it an indissoluble partnership—but not a partnership superimposed upon one nation by another. Hence you find . . . that the Congress claims that either party should have the right to sever the connection, to dissolve the partnership.'[31] As for the words 'dominion status' or 'complete independence', he did not care. 'Call it by any name you like,' he said, 'a rose will smell as sweet by another name, but it must be the rose of liberty that I want and not the artificial product.'[32]

Although Gandhi continued to say until 1939 that he would be satisfied with dominion status for India,[33] he had, ever since 1931,[34] begun to veer round gradually, almost reluctantly, to the view of Andrews and Jawaharlal Nehru, that the concept of dominion status was not applicable to India for the simple reason that India was not a daughter nation. The definition of 'dominion' by enumeration in the Statute of Westminster, the deliberate avoidance of the term 'dominion status' in the Government of India Act of 1935, and the fact that the British Commonwealth still comprised white members only—all served to deepen this impression. Nor could he fail to note that the vast majority of Indian nationalists was allergic to that idea. When, therefore, during the Second World War, the British government made offers of dominion status to India at the end of hostilities, Gandhi advised them to talk of independence and not of dominion status.[35] It was not until 1946 that the British government appreciated his point. But even when Gandhi became a convert to the idea of independence, he never failed to assert that he visualized nothing but the closest and friendliest relations between an independent India and Great Britain. And inasmuch as the Commonwealth connexion was in the Indian mind synonymous with the connexion with Great Britain, Gandhi's conversion was not of much consequence.

A Friendly Foe

Gandhi—'the opponent of British rule in India, who yet understood and even loved the English people'[36]—was the strangest rebel the world has ever known. Day in and day out for thirty years, he told his countrymen that they should regard Englishmen as their friends and not enemies, that their fight was against the system and not against the men administering it, and that in so far as they failed to understand this distinction they harmed their own cause. Even a man like Jawaharlal Nehru, who did not stand much in need of such preaching, admitted its corrective effect in his life and thinking.[37] It is rare for a nationalist leader to avow openly and unceasingly that he had been and remained 'a sincere friend' of the country against which he was waging a non-violent war. Nor was it insignificant that his war was non-violent. Competent English observers have testified that Gandhi, by bringing the Indian revolutionary movement into the open, freed it from secret, terroristic activities and rid the English of the 'Mutiny complex'.[38] Had the Indian nationalist movement turned violent, it would have in its turn invited violent repression, and ended by leaving a legacy of bloodshed, which would have been extremely hard to overcome. If there was no 'Mutiny' or 'Amritsar' after 1919, and if the transfer of power in India in 1947 could be 'a treaty of peace without a war', credit is as much due to Gandhi's leadership as to enlightened British policy.

Gandhi did not allow Indian nationalism to become narrow, racial and isolationist. He tried his best to save the Congress from getting into the strait-jacket of secession and republicanism. He gave it the right leaders. He consistently opposed those who stood for a total break with Britain and advocated the setting-up of a parallel government in India. He forced the separatists in India to argue their case on a high moral level, free from distorting emotion and prejudice. He never looked for outside help to free India. He kept the quarrel between England and India, what it was in essentials, a family quarrel. 'I know the English and they know may ours in a deadly but friendly struggle,' he was fond of telling foreigners.

In the final stages of the negotiations which led to the transfer of power in India in 1947, Gandhi did not play a major role, but the settlement on the basis of dominion status had his blessings. He called it 'the noblest act of the British nation'.[39] 'The British', he told his prayer audience on 28 September 1947, 'rose to the occasion, decided voluntarily to break the empire, and erect, in its place, an unseen and more glorious empire of hearts.'[40]

Gandhi and the Commonwealth

Why did Gandhi value India's continued association with the Commonwealth? He was no narrow patriot. He never wanted India to live the life of 'a frog in the well'. Isolation was neither practicable nor desirable. Gandhi felt that it would be ridiculous for a free India to develop new contacts and relationships with the outside world, while at the same time severing old, established ones. His partiality for the British was pronounced. 'I am an admirer of the Birtish character,' he remarked to a French friend in 1947.[41] When Horace Alexander told him shortly before his death, 'I think you are more pro-British than I am', Gandhi replied, 'You may well say that'.[42] He shared the belief of his political 'guru', G.K. Gokhale, that the union of Britain and India was intended on high to fulfil some great purpose for the benefit of mankind. He looked upon India's association with the Commonwealth as the symbol and instrument of a wider international system, and as one likely to promote the cause of freedom and peace. He sought an equal and honourable partnership for India with Britain, he told the Round Table Conference in 1931, 'not merely for the benefit of India, and not merely for mutual benefit, [but] in order that the great weight that is crushing the world . . . may be lifted from its shoulders'.[43]

In 1931 Gandhi had told the British people that he wanted India to share the sorrows and misfortunes of Britain to the fullest extent; 'Yes, if need be, but at her own will, to fight side by side with Britain, not for the exploitation of a single human being on earth, but it may be conceivably for the good of the whole world'.[44] Had he and the Congress been properly tackled by the British government and had a satisfactory solution of the Indian problem been found, it is not unreasonable to surmise—especially in view of his declared sympathy for the Allied cause, that Gandhi would have overcome his pacifist scruples and supported India's co-operation with Britain in World War II. His statements in 1946 and 1947 indicate that he would not have objected to India entering into defensive military arrangements with Britain.[45]

The idea of India and Pakistan—both members of the Commonwealth—being at war was abhorrent to him. 'The Dominions must not be enemies one of the other. The Dominions of the Commonwealth cannot be enemies of one another,' he remarked in 1947.[46] It is well known that he was opposed to the move of the Indian government to take the Kashmir dispute to the United Nations and instead favoured its settlement either through bilateral talks or British good offices. It is also interesting to note that he had been insistent that some provision for the joint defence of India and Pakistan should be made before the partition was effected.[47]

Gandhi always admired the British people for their sense of tradition and was anxious not to hurt it in any way. In July 1947, he 'heard with sorrow' that the Union Jack was not to occupy a place on the Indian national flag: 'The retention of the Union Jack, for such period as India was a Dominion was in his opinion a point of honour....He was solicitous about their [British] traditions.'[48] He retained his regard for British royalty till the end of his life. In 1947 on the occasion of Queen (then Princess) Elizabeth's marriage he sent her as a gift a table-cloth, prepared of yarn spun by himself.

Gandhi had hoped that with the emergence of India as a free and equal member of the Commonwealth the principle of racial equality would stand finally vindicated, and that South Africa would be persuaded to recognize it. What would have been his attitude towards the South African question today is anybody's guess. An interesting fact may, however, be recalled here. Of all Commonwealth statesmen, Gandhi had probably the greatest admiration and respect for General Smuts, and the latter reciprocated his feelings.[49] What more, one wonders, had these two great men in common, besides their faith in the Commonwealth ideal? The modern Commonwealth owes much to Smuts and Gandhi. It is sad to think that South Africa, one of whose greatest sons was Smuts, and where Gandhi discovered himself and his technique of *satyagraha*, should have chosen to leave the Commonwealth. All of us who feel unhappy over South Africa's withdrawal from the Commonwealth, but more so over the calculated persistence of her present rulers in their unjust and anachronistic policy of *apartheid*, would have often wished that Gandhi and Smuts were here today to fight their war and to make their peace again for the good of that country and the Commonwealth.

8

NEHRU AND THE COMMONWEALTH

Independent India's decision in 1949 to remain a member of the British Commonwealth—even after the Indian Constituent Assembly had on 22 January 1947 declared its 'firm and solemn resolve to proclaim India as an Independent Sovereign Republic'[1]—came as a surprise to many people in India and abroad, more so because this decision was taken by a government headed by Jawaharlal Nehru, who since the late 1920s had been a bitter opponent of the idea of dominion status and an ardent advocate of complete independence for his country. In this paper I shall try to answer two interrelated questions: first, why did Nehru decide in 1949 to keep India in the Commonwealth? and, second, what did the Commonwealth mean to Nehru?

In the 1920s and 1930s Nehru considered the very idea of a vast and ancient country like India remaining a dominion of England to be ridiculous and humiliating. He did not believe in reforming imperialism by entering into a partnership with it. He was firmly of the view that the British Commonwealth, in spite of its high sounding name, did not stand for true international co-operation. It was an exclusive system whose membership would deprive India of the freedom to develop contacts with the world at large, especially with the other countries of Asia. He did not stand for a narrow, isolated nationalism, but he felt that a true commonwealth of nations could not grow out of the British Empire.[2]

Nehru was a severe critic of British foreign policy in the 1920s and 1930s, particularly as witnessed in Britain's dealings with the countries of the Middle East, with China, and with Fascist Italy and Nazi Germany. He denounced Britain as the greatest enemy of national freedom, of disarmament and peace throughout the world. One of his great objections to dominion status for India was that it would mean the involvement of India in the reactionary foreign policy of Great Britain. He regarded Britain as 'the archpriest of imperialism' and India as the pivot of her imperial policy. In order to retain her hold on India, Britain had subjugated the other parts of Africa and Asia. Indian soldiers had been used to do 'the dirty work of British imperialism'. The independence of India would, Nehru argued, be a death-blow to British imperialism and the signal for the liberation of other oppressed nationalities.[3]

It was the Lahore session of the Indian National Congress, presided over by Jawaharlal Nehru, which on 31 December 1929 defined the word 'Swaraj' in the Congress constitution to mean 'Complete Independence'.[4] Nehru and Mahatma Gandhi jointly drafted the 'Independence Day Pledge' which Congressmen repeated year after year from 26 January 1930 onwards and which, among other things, said: 'The British Government in India has not only deprived the Indian people of their freedom but has based itself on the exploitation of the masses, and has ruined India economically, politically, culturally, and spiritually. We believe, therefore, that India must sever the British connection and attain Purna Swaraj or complete independence.'[5]

Like most leading Indian nationalists Nehru was a keen observer of developments in other parts of the British Empire. In 1933 he surveyed the developments within the British Empire since the Anglo-Irish Treaty of 1921 in a letter to his daughter, Indira: 'The formation of the Irish Free State led to some far-reaching consequences in Britain's imperial policies. The Irish treaty had given Ireland a greater measure of independence than was possessed at the time, in law, by the other Dominions. As soon as Ireland got this, the other Dominions automatically took it also, and the idea of Dominion status underwent a change. Further changes in the direction of greater independence of the Dominions followed some Imperial Conferences which were held between England and the Dominions. Ireland, with her strong republican movement, was always pulling towards complete independence. So also was South Africa with her Boer majority. In this way the position of the Dominions went on changing and improving till they came to be considered as sister-nations with England in the British Commonwealth of Nations. This sounds fine, and no doubt it does represent a progressive growth towards an equal political status. But the equality is more in theory than in fact. Economically the Dominions are tied to Britain and British capital, and there are many ways of bringing economic pressure to bear on them. At the same time as the Dominions grow, their economic interests tend to conflict with those of England. Thus the Empire gets weaker. It was because of this imminent danger of the cracking up of the Empire that England agreed to the loosening of the bonds and admitting political equality with the Dominions. By wisely going thus far in time, she saved much. But not for long. The forces that separate the Dominions from England continue to work; they are in the main economic forces. It was because of this, as well as the undoubted decline of England, that I wrote to you of the fading away of the British Empire. If it is difficult for the Dominions to remain tied to England for long, with all their common traditions and culture and racial unity, how much more difficult must it be for India to remain tied to her- For India's economic interests come into direct conflict with British interests, and one of them must bow to the other. Thus a free India is most unlikely to accept this connection, with its corollary of subordinating her economic policy to that of Britain.'[6]

Writing in *Vendredi* of Paris in 1936, Nehru remarked: 'Some people imagine that India may develop into a free dominion of the British group of nations like Canada or Australia. This seems to be a fantastic idea. Even the existing dominions, in spite of their numerous links with Great Britain, are gradually drifting apart as their economic interests conflict. The drift is greatest in the case of Ireland, partly for historical reasons, and South Africa. There are few natural links between India and England, and there is a historical and ever-growing hostility between them. In many parts of the Empire there is racial ill-treatment and a policy of exclusion of Indians. But more important still, there is a conflict of economic interests. So long as India is controlled by the British Government this conflict is resolved in favour of Britain, but the moment India becomes a real dominion the two will pull in different ways and a break would become inevitable, if the present capitalist order survives till then. There is another interesting aspect of this question. India, by virtue of her size, population, and potential wealth, is far the most important member of the British Empire. So long as the rest of the Empire exploits her, she remains on the imperial fringe. But a free India in the British group of nations would inevitably tend to become the centre of gravity of that group; Delhi might challenge London as the nerve centre of the Empire. That position would become intolerable for England as well as the white dominions. They would prefer to have India outside their group, an independent but friendly country, rather than be boss of their own household.'[7]

But even while inveighing against the British Empire and the idea of dominion status for India, Nehru never forgot to emphasize that the Indian nationalist movement was not directed against Britain or the British people. 'Our quarrel is not with the people of England but with the imperialism of England,' he said. 'The day England sheds her imperialism,' he affirmed, 'we shall gladly co-operate with her.' India could have no truck with British imperialism. Nor could she have 'a real measure of freedom within the limits of the British Empire'. 'Before a new bridge is built', he insisted, 'on the basis of friendship and co-operation, the present chains which tie us to England must be severed. Only then can real co-operation take place.'[8]

Presiding over the Lahore session of the Indian National Congress in 1929 Nehru had remarked: 'Independence for us means complete freedom from British domination and British imperialism. Having attained our freedom, I have no doubt that India will welcome all attempts at world co-operation and federation, and will even agree to give up part of her own independence to a larger group of which she is an equal member.' He had reiterated his opposition to dominion status, but left the door open to friendship with Britain: 'India could never be an equal member of the Commonwealth unless imperialism and all it implies is discarded.'[9]

Jawaharlal Nehru was the most internationally-minded of Indians. Not only was he free from narrow nationalism, he had no bitterness against the British people as such. As he wrote in his *Autobiography* in the mid-1930s: 'It is not a question of an implacable and irreconcilable antagonism to England and the English people, or the desire to break from them at all costs. It would be natural enough if there was bad blood between India and England after what has happened. "The clumsiness of power spoils the key and uses the pick-axe," says Tagore, and the key to our hearts was destroyed long ago, and the abundant use of the pick-axe on us has not made us partial to the British. But if we claim to serve the larger cause of India and humanity we cannot afford to be carried away by our momentary passions. And even if we were so inclined the hard training which Gandhiji has given us for the last fifteen years would prevent us. I write this sitting in a British prison and for months past my mind has been full of anxiety, and I have perhaps suffered more during this solitary imprisonment than I have done in gaol before. Anger and resentment have often filled my mind at various happenings, and yet as I sit here, and look deep into my mind and heart, I do not find any anger against England or the British people. I dislike British imperialism and I resent its imposition on India; I dislike the capitalist system; I dislike exceedingly and resent the way India is exploited by the ruling classes of Britain. But I do not hold England or the English people as a whole responsible for this, and even if I did, I do not think it would make much difference, for it is a little foolish to lose one's temper at or condemn a whole people. They are as much the victims of circumstances as we are.

'Personally, I owe too much to England in my mental make-up ever to feel wholly alien to her. And, do what I will, I cannot get rid of the habits of mind, and the standards and ways of judging other countries as well as life generally, which I acquired at school and college in England. All my predilections (apart from the political plane) are in favour of England and the English people, and if I have become what is called an uncompromising opponent of British rule in India, it is almost in spite of myself.

'It is that rule, that domination, to which we object, and with which we cannot compromise willingly—not the English people. Let us by all means have the closest contacts with the English and other foreign peoples. We want fresh air in India, fresh and vital ideas, healthy co-operation; we have grown too musty with age. But if the English come in the role of a tiger they can expect no friendship or co-operation....

'Indian freedom and British imperialism are two incompatibles, and neither martial law nor all the sugar-coating in the world can make them compatible or bring them together. Only with the elimination of imperialism from India will conditions be created which permit of real Indo-British co-operation.'[10]

Nehru's avowed partiality for England and the English appears to have received a temporary set-back in the late 1930s and the early 1940s. He intensely disliked the British policy of appeasing

Fascism and Nazism. He was shocked and hurt by the brutal manner in which the British government suppressed the 'Quit India' movement in 1942. While imprisoned in the Ahmednagar Fort—incidentally, Nehru's longest ever imprisonment—he wrote in *The Discovery of India* in 1944: 'I had always looked forward in the past to a visit to England, because I have many friends there and old memories draw me. But now I found that there was no such desire and the idea was distasteful. I wanted to keep as far away from England as possible, and I had no wish even to discuss India's problems with Englishmen. And then I remembered some friends and softened a little, and I told myself how wrong it was to judge a whole people in this way. I thought also of the terrible experiences that the English people had gone through in this war, of the continuous strain in which they had lived, of the loss of so many of their loved ones. All this helped to tone down my feelings, but this basic reaction remained. Probably time and the future will lessen it and give another perspective.'[11]

Time and the future did lessen Nehru's adverse reaction and gave him another perspective. Post-war Britain obviously aroused Nehru's sympathy and admiration. She had fought and suffered in the cause of democracy and freedom. Immediately after victory had been achieved on the western front she had rejected Winston Churchill and the Tories and voted a Labour government to power with Clement Attlee as prime minister. And Attlee and his colleagues lost no time in applying themselves to the task of translating into reality the policy, which they had long advocated, of giving independence to India.

As one examines Nehru's utterances in the year immediately preceding the transfer of power on 15 August 1947 one notices a gradual but discernible trend in his thinking towards the maintenance of friendly relations with Britain and the Commonwealth. Speaking as head of the newly-formed interim government, Nehru remarked on 27 September 1946: 'In spite of our past history of conflict, we hope that an independent India will have friendly and co-operative relations with England and the countries of the British Commonwealth.'[12] Again, on 15 December 1946, while moving the 'Objectives Resolution' in the Indian Constituent Assembly, he said: 'We want to make friends, in spite of the long history of conflict in the past, with England also.' He referred to his recent and disappointing visit to England in connexion with the deadlock over the Cabinet Mission proposals, but added: '...we seek the co-operation of England, even at this stage, when we are full of suspicion of each other. We feel that if that co-operation is denied, it will be injurious to India, certainly to some extent, probably more so to England, and, to some extent, to the world at large.'[13] Once again, on 22 January 1947, while replying to the debate on the 'Objectives Resolution' in the Indian Constituent Assembly, Nehru observed: 'Now, what relation will... [the future Indian] Republic bear to the other countries of the world, to England and to the British Commonwealth and the rest? For a long time past we have taken a pledge on Independence Day that India must sever her connection with Great Britain, because that connection had become an emblem of British domination. At no time have we ever thought in terms of isolating ourselves in this part of the world from other countries or of being hostile to countries which have dominated over us. On the eve of this great occasion, when we stand on the threshold of freedom, we do not wish to carry a trail of hostility with us against any other country. We want to be friendly to all. We want to be friendly with the British people and the British Commonwealth of Nations.... If we seek to be [a] free, independent, democratic Republic, it is not to dissociate ourselves from other countries, but rather as a free nation to co-operate in the fullest measure with other countries for peace and freedom, to co-operate with Britain, with the British Commonwealth of Nations, with the United States of America, with the Soviet Union, and with all other countries big and small. But real co-operation would only come between us and these other nations when we know that we are free to co-operate and are not imposed upon and forced to co-operate. As long as there is the slightest trace of compulsion, there can be no co-operation.'[14]

Thus it is clear that even before the transfer of power in August 1947—in fact, even before the Attlee declaration of 20 February 1947 regarding 'the transference of power into responsible Indian hands by a date not later than June 1948',[15] or the arrival of Lord Mountbatten as viceroy in India in March 1947—Nehru was inclined to keep India in the Commonwealth. The manner in which the British transferred power in August 1947 undoubtedly created a favourable impression on the minds of Nehru and his associates and reinforced their desire to let India remain in the

Commonwealth. Nehru's friendship with the Mountbattens certainly strengthened his resolve and eased the process by which a republican India stayed in the Commonwealth. But the fact cannot be over-emphasized that already in late 1946 and early 1947 Nehru's thoughts were tending in the direction of maintaining friendly relations with Britain and the Commonwealth.

There were many Indians and Britons who thought that the resolution of the Indian Constituent Assembly of 22 January 1947, which had declared that India would become an 'Independent Sovereign Republic', had already prejudged the issue of Commonwealth membership, for a republican India could not remain in the Commonwealth. This was not Nehru's view. He repeatedly stated that 'this business of our being a republic' had 'little or nothing to do with what relations we should have with other countries, notably with the United Kingdom or the Commonwealth', and that India's membership of the Commonwealth was 'something apart from and in a sense independent of the Constitution' that she adopted.[16] Nehru was encouraged in this belief by the fact that Eire, though a republic in all but name since 1937, had continued as a member of the Commonwealth.[17]

The fact that Nehru and other Indian leaders accepted the transfer of power in August 1947 on the dominion-status basis, albeit as a temporary arrangement in order to facilitate a speedy changeover, was not without some significance. It indicated that he and his associates recognized that the concept of dominion status had changed and that it now meant virtually complete independence. It also indicated that they were not averse to the idea of India remaining in the British Commonwealth. More significantly, it left independent India in the British Commonwealth.

Discussing the probable reasons which prompted India to remain in the Commonwealth, Professor Nicholas Mansergh writes: 'There was, however, one immediate factor which may well have been decisive. Pakistan was committed to Commonwealth membership. If India seceded, did not that, in view especially of pre-partition disputes on division of assets, evacuee property, river water and above all Kashmir, mean the likelihood of an anti-Indian Commonwealth?'[18] It is true that Indian leaders were anxious that Muslim League (later Pakistani) politicians should not be allowed to make political capital out of their loudly proclaimed intention to stay in the Commonwealth. Many Indian leaders were even apprehensive that if India went out of and Pakistan remained in the Commonwealth, Pakistan might become a base of British imperialism. They were also advised by their British friends that the best way of neutralizing anti-Indian elements in Britain and the Commonwealth—and these were not insubstantial—was that India should remain in the Commonwealth.[19] But until we have access to the papers of Nehru—both private and official—which are still closed to the public, we shall not be able to judge precisely how much the thought of using the Commonwealth membership 'as a counterpoise to Pakistan'[20] weighed with Nehru in his calculation of India's self-interest while deciding to keep India in the Commonwealth.

It was as prime minister of the dominion of India that Nehru first attended the meeting of Commonwealth prime ministers in London in October 1948. Personal experience further convinced him of the value of the Commonwealth connexion. In a broadcast from London on 26 October 1948 he spoke of the old colonial empire of Britain gradually changing into a combination of free dominions and non-self-governing countries and expressed the hope that 'this changeover will be complete soon so that the Commonwealth of Nations will become a real commonwealth of free nations'. He referred to the mutual understanding that resulted from the meeting and added: 'We may not agree about everything, but it was surprising what a large measure of unanimity there was, not only in the objectives to be aimed at, but also in the methods to be pursued.... This meeting has shown me that there is great scope for the Commonwealth to function in this way, and not only to help itself but to help others also.'[21]

On his return from London, Nehru, speaking in the Indian Constituent Assembly on 8 November 1948, alluded to the private and unofficial discussions he had with other Commonwealth prime ministers regarding India's continued membership of the Commonwealth and remarked that he had made it clear to them that India 'desired to be associated in friendly relationship with other countries, with the United Kingdom and the Commonwealth' even after becoming a republic, but how this could be done was a matter for careful consideration by all concerned.[22]

The Congress party endorsed Nehru's stand. Meeting in its annual session at Jaipur, it passed a resolution on 18 December 1948, which, among other things, said: 'In view of the attainment of complete independence and the establishment of the Republic of India which will symbolize that independence and give to India the status among the nations of the world that is her rightful due, her present association with the United Kingdom and the Commonwealth of Nations will necessarily have to change. India, however, desires to maintain all such links with other countries as do not come in the way of her freedom of action and independence, and the Congress would welcome her free association with the independent nations of the Commonwealth for their common weal and the promotion of world peace.'[23]

After months of consultation and deliberation a formula was evolved which permitted India, if and when she became a republic, to remain a member of the Commonwealth, without damaging the monarchical basis of the other members, or destroying the common bond of the Crown on which the Commonwealth was built. The future Indian Republic would owe no allegiance to the Crown, nor would the Monarch have any place in her government. She would, however, remain a full member of the Commonwealth and would acknowledge the King as a symbol of the free association of its independent member nations; and, as such, the Head of the Commonwealth.[24] The formula was accepted by the Commonwealth prime ministers at their meeting in London in late April 1949.[25] It was approved both by the Indian Constituent Assembly[26] and by the Congress party[27] in May 1949.

The settlement of April 1949 was, as Professor Mansergh has rightly pointed out, specific, not general, in application.[28] There was no decision that a republic as such could be a full member of the Commonwealth. But the exception soon became a category and later the majority of the Asian and African Commonwealth states opted to follow the same course.

In any discussion of the reasons which prompted Nehru to decide in 1949 that India should continue to stay in the Commonwealth we must not also lose sight of the following important facts. When India became independent in 1947, she had been a member of the Commonwealth for thirty years, having been admitted to the Imperial Conference in 1917.[29] The decision that India had therefore to make on achieving independence was not whether to join the Commonwealth or not, but whether to remain in the Commonwealth or leave it. Though the Indian Constituent Assembly had already, on 22 January 1947, declared its 'firm and solemn resolve to proclaim India as an Independent Sovereign Republic', the government of independent India wisely suspended its judgement on the question of Commonwealth membership until 1949—unlike Burma which decided to stay out of the Commonwealth immediately after gaining independence. This suspension of judgement for two years by India was made possible by the fact that India was already in the Commonwealth. It was very fortunate, for it gave India and the other members of the Commonwealth time to think over the problem and to prepare for the necessary adjustments. It also enabled Nehru to attend the Commonwealth Prime Ministers' Conference in London in October 1948, where he had the opportunity of seeing things from the inside and of becoming convinced that the Commonwealth was a free association of equal nations, in no way subordinate one to another, and that 'membership in the Commonwealth meant independence plus, not independence minus'.[30] Had India not already attained her special status in the Commonwealth in 1917, it is doubtful whether she would have chosen to remain a member in 1949, and also whether the other members of the Commonwealth would so readily have accepted her, especially as a republic.

India's continued association with the Commonwealth was also made possible by the manner in which the Indian nationalist movement was conducted and the way the British responded to it. The inevitable bitterness created by the nationalist movement and its periodical repression did not fail to colour Indian patriotism with a strong antipathy to their rulers; it was intensified by a distrust of British intentions, and in the minds of many Indians the sense of subjection bit so deep that they wanted, as it were, to cut themselves away from their past by severing all relations with Britain. They demanded that the Indian National Congress—the party which led the Indian freedom movement—should commit itself to secession from the British Commonwealth. But some of the leaders of the Congress—chief among whom was Mahatma Gandhi—consistently opposed this demand. Gandhi argued that if Britain offered India an equal and honourable partnership, it would be 'petulant', 'vindictive' and 'religiously unlawful' on India's part to refuse it. 'The better mind of the world desires today,' he told the Congress in 1924, 'not absolutely independent states warring against one another, but a federation of friendly interdependent states. The consummation of that event may be far off. I want to make no grand claim for our country. But I see nothing grand or impossible about our expressing our readiness for universal interdependence. It should rest with Britain to say that she will have no real alliance with India. I desire the ability to be totally independent without asserting the independence. Any scheme that I would frame, while Britain declares her goal about India to be complete equality within the Empire, would be that of alliance and not of independence without alliance.'[31]

When in 1929 the Congress rejected—much to Gandhi's distaste—the ideal of dominion status for India in favour of 'Complete Independence', Gandhi saw to it that the Congress was not committed to secession from the British Commonwealth.[32] At the Round Table Conference in London in 1931 he remarked: 'The Congress contemplates a connection with the British people—but that connection to be such as can exist between two absolute equals—I have aspired—I still aspire—to be a citizen, not in the Empire, but in a Commonwealth; in a partnership if possible—if God wills it an indissoluble partnership—but not a partnership superimposed upon one nation by another. Hence you find that the Congress claims that either party should have the right to sever the connection, to dissolve the partnership.'[33] Gandhi did not allow Indian nationalism to become narrow, violent, racial and isolationist. He saved the Congress from getting into the straitjacket of secession. He never sought outside help to free India. He kept the quarrel between India and England what it was in essentials, a family quarrel. 'I know the English and they know me; ours is a deadly but friendly struggle,' he was fond of telling foreign visitors. It is rare for a nationalist leader to avow openly and incessantly—as Gandhi did—that he had been and remained a sincere friend of the country against which he was waging a non-violent war. Nor was it insignificant that his war was non-violent. Had the Indian nationalist movement turned violent, it would in its turn have invited violent repression, and ended by leaving a legacy of bloodshed, which would have been (as the examples of Ireland and South Africa prove) extremely hard to overcome. If the transfer of power in India in 1947 could be what Lord Samuel called it, 'a treaty of peace without a war',[31] credit is due as much to Gandhi's leadership as to enlightened British policy.

It can well be argued that Britain was often too slow and grudging in making political concessions to Indians. But she never adopted an attitude of uncompromising hostility to Indian political aspirations. Concessions were periodically made to Indians—if only just in time—and what is more important, they were actually made to moderate-minded Indians. This kept alive the faith of many Indians in British good intentions, strengthened the hands of the moderates against the extremists in India, and prevented the drift of the Indian nationalist movement towards violence. British policy in India thus differed essentially from that in Ireland, where concessions had to be made to extremism and violence long after they had been denied to moderation and reason.

Probably nothing became the British in India so much like leaving it. The timing and manner of the transfer of power in India made a profound impression on the Indian mind. 'The British had set an example of voluntary withdrawal with grace. They had been magnanimous. Shall India be mean and petty, and continue nursing old wrongs? No, she must also rise to the occasion and set an example of magnanimity by clasping the extended hand of the erstwhile adversary.' This is how Nehru and many other Indian leaders argued. Describing the feelings which were uppermost in his mind when he decided to continue India's membership of the Commonwealth in 1949, Nehru remarked: 'I wanted the world to see that India was prepared to co-operate even with those with whom she had been fighting in the past....'[35]

Another reason—and this was perhaps the most important—which persuaded Nehru to keep India in the Commonwealth in 1949 was that there was a Labour government in Britain at that time. The Labour party contained many old friends of India. It had supported the cause of Indian self-government over the years. It had given India independence and redeemed its promise. It wanted India to remain in the Commonwealth, but gave her freedom to remain or quit. All these things were important. There was —and remains—in India a deep and long-standing dislike of the Conservatives. Had there been a Conservative government in Britain in 1947 or 1949, it is very doubtful whether India would have remained in the Commonwealth. The Labour government granted Indians what they had been demanding ever since 1920— the right to secede from the Commonwealth. It was the denial of this right in the past which prejudiced opinion in Ireland against the Commonwealth connexion. It was the denial of this right which was the cause of so many attacks upon the Commonwealth membership in India during the 1920s and the 1930s. It is significant that soon after 1942—when the right to secede from the Commonwealth was first explicitly conceded in the famous Cripps proposals of that year[36] prejudice against the Commonwealth connexion lessened in India. On the question of the Crown, Nehru and other Indian leaders were prepared for a give-and-take. If the Commonwealth was willing to retain a republican India, they did not mind recognizing 'the King as the symbol of the free association of its independent member nations and as such the Head of the Commonwealth'.

Nehru knew that the Commonwealth had changed and was changing and that it was no longer a western or Anglo-Saxon club. He rightly judged that the Commonwealth would grow and that in the course of time there would be many more Asian and African countries in it, and that India's membership of the Commonwealth would facilitate this development.[37]

Nehru was a liberal-internationalist, not an isolationist. He did not want India to live the life of 'a frog in the well'. He was conscious of India's important position in the world. He was inspired by the conviction that India, having come to her own, had a distinct contribution to make to international problems. He was eager to develop new relationships with the outside world and he felt that it would look ridiculous for India to sever old, established ties with Britain and the Commonwealth while trying to establish new ones. The Commonwealth, he rightly reasoned, not only offered India an established network of international relationships which it would be foolish on her part to throw away, but could also help her in developing new contacts.[38]

Immediately after independence India was faced with tremendous problems. There were the ill effects of partition. There was the problem of the Indian princely states, and especially of Hyderabad and Kashmir.[39] Her defences were weak. She was new to the international community. She had few friends in Asia. Her experience of the Asian Relations Conference held at Delhi in March 1947 had not been very encouraging. Her relations with Pakistan and the Soviet Union were far from being cordial. In a note written in 1948, Sir B.N. Rau, then constitutional adviser to the Indian government, argued that 'this is no time for leaving the Commonwealth and venturing into the unknown, for she [India] may thereby create for herself a new set of problems even more baffling'.[40] Nehru emphasized the same point in 1949. He said: 'If we dissociate ourselves completely from the Commonwealth, then for the moment we are completely isolated. We cannot remain completely isolated, and so inevitably by stress of circumstances we have to incline in some direction or other. But that inclination in some direction or other will necessarily be on a basis of give-and-take. It may be in the nature of alliances: you give something yourself and get something in return. In other words, it may involve commitments far more than at present. There are no commitments today.'[41] Membership of the Commonwealth gave India friends and a sense of security and stability in the difficult early years of her freedom.

Justifying his government's decision to continue India's membership of the Commonwealth, Nehru remarked in the Indian Constituent Assembly on 16 May 1949 that it was 'beneficial to us and to certain causes in the world that we wish to advance'.[42] Of the benefits to India there could be little doubt. There were the advantages of co-operation in the economic and political fields, in education and diplomacy, and even in defence. The bulk of India's trade was then with the Commonwealth; her foreign exchange reserves were tied up in the Sterling area; there were substantial communities of Indian settlers in various parts of the British Empire;[43] her armed forces depended on British-made weapons; she had a common concern with the Commonwealth in the defence of the Indian Ocean area and in the maintenance of a balance of power in the whole Eurasian continent.

What of the larger causes in the world that Nehru wished to advance? Let us first see what were these causes which he had at heart. They were peace, freedom for colonial peoples, the fight against racialism, international co-operation, especially co-operation with Asian and African nations, and raising the living standards of under-developed countries. All these causes, Nehru thought, India could serve better by remaining in the Commonwealth, and he has been proved right.

As Professor Nicholas Mansergh rightly observes, 'Nehru re-interpreted the idea of the Commonwealth to fit his own philosophy of international relations.'[44] He viewed the Commonwealth as an association of governments and peoples brought together by history and maintained for the promotion of certain common interests and ideals. It was a bridge between east and west, between various continents, races and cultures, a grouping of friendly nations making widely differing responses to the cold war, and thus cutting across the frozen configuration of international politics. It was an instrument of peace. It brought 'a touch of healing'[15] to an embittered world. It was something of an example to the world of the Gandhian principles applied to relations between nations.[46]

Nehru did not consider the Commonwealth to be a super-state or even the embryo of such a state. He believed that the Commonwealth was a free association of sovereign states and that it could only survive as such. He was opposed to all proposals for giving the Commonwealth supra-national authority as being misconceived and potentially dangerous. He would not allow the Commonwealth to interfere in the domestic affairs of any member nation. He objected to the setting up of a Commonwealth tribunal or to the Commonwealth assuming mediatory responsibilities in intra-Commonwealth disputes. Replying to the criticism in India that he had failed to raise the issue of racial discrimination by the South African government at the Commonwealth Prime Ministers' Conference, Nehru remarked in May 1949: 'It was a dangerous thing for us to bring that matter within the purview of the Commonwealth. Because then the very thing to which you and I object might have taken place. That is, the Commonwealth might have been considered as some kind of a superior body which sometimes acts as a tribunal, or judges, or in a sense supervises, the activities of its member nations. That certainly would have meant a diminution in our independence and sovereignty, if we had once accepted that principle. Therefore, we were not prepared and we are not prepared to treat the Commonwealth as such or even to bring disputes between member nations of the Commonwealth before the Commonwealth body. We may, of course, in a friendly way discuss the matter; that is a different matter.'[47] Consistent with this view, Nehru resolutely opposed the raising of the Indo-Pakistani dispute over Kashmir at the Commonwealth Prime Ministers' Conference in London in 1951, but agreed to talk about it informally with interested prime ministers outside the forum of the Conference.[48]

Nehru did not regard the Commonwealth as a political bloc. In fact he decided to keep India in the Commonwealth because it was not a political bloc and because he did not wish her to join any one of the existing political blocs. Though he was anxious to promote greater understanding, co-operation and agreement among members of the Commonwealth, he did not think that the Commonwealth could have a common foreign policy. He believed that any attempt to have uniform policies among Commonwealth countries—so differently conditioned, both geographically and historically—was doomed to failure, and that a friendly approach and the desire to consult and co-operate with each other were more important than an artificial unity in policy.

Nehru valued the Commonwealth as a friendly association that neither circumscribed India's political and constitutional independence nor came in the way of her pursuing her own independent policies in international affairs. As he said in 1950: 'Presumably, some people imagine that our association with the Commonwealth imposes some kind of restricting or limiting factor upon our activities, be they political, economic, foreign, domestic or anything else. In the case of the United Nations or the International Monetary Fund, some limiting factors certainly come in, as they must, if we join an international organization of that type; but in our association with the Commonwealth, there is not the least vestige of such a limiting factor.... We may carry out any policy we like regardless of whether we are in the Commonwealth or not.'[49] The Commonwealth represented a form of international co-operation which, according to Nehru, suited India best, being intimate and informal, beneficial and yet not binding. In 1956 Nehru remarked: 'Of all the types of associations we have between nations, probably this rather invisible type of association is stronger than alliances or treaties.' He would like to see, he added, a world develop in which all the nations were associated in some such friendly way with each other.[50] But while membership of the Commonwealth did not bind or commit India in any way, it certainly exposed her to other influences. This, however, in Nehru's view was neither a disadvantage nor a one-way traffic. 'When people think of the Commonwealth influencing us in our policies,' he remarked in 1950, 'may I suggest to them the possibility that we may also greatly influence others in the right direction?'[51]

Nehru prized the Commonwealth machinery for the exchange of information and opinion. He valued the Commonwealth for its technical assistance, educational facilities and trading privileges. But great as these advantages were, they were not in Nehru's opinion decisive. Membership of the Commonwealth, according to Nehru, had been most useful to India in that it had allowed her to pursue policies which were dear to her heart, and to exercise a greater influence in the world than she would have otherwise done. It had enabled her to aid the transformation of the Commonwealth in a direction which she favoured. It had helped her to develop closer contacts with countries in Asia and Africa. It had saved her from the distasteful necessity in the modern world of leaning too heavily on one super-power or the other. It had helped her to remain independent and non-aligned, and to reach out and influence opinion in all parts of the world.[52]

BIOGRAPHICAL NOTES

ABRAHAMS, LIONEL (1869-1918). Entered India Office 1898; assistant under-secretary 1911-17.

ALEXANDER, HORACE GUNDRY (1899-   ). A prominent Quaker; author and teacher.

AMERY, L.C.M.S. (1873-1955). Conservative M. P. 1911-45; first lord of admiralty 1922-3; colonial secretary 1924-9; secretary of state for India 1940-5.

ANDREWS, C. F. (1871-1940). Joined Cambridge brotherhood in Delhi 1904; teacher, author and social reformer.

ASQUITH, HERBERT HENRY, FIRST EARL OF OXFORD AND ASQUITH (1852-1928). Liberal statesman; home secretary 1892-5; chancellor of exchequer 1905-8; prime minister of Britain 1908-16; created earl 1925.

ATTLEE, C. R., FIRST EARL (1883-1967). Labour M. P. 1922-55; under-secretary for war 1924; member of Indian statutory commission 1927-30; prime minister of Britain 1945-51.

BALFOUR, ARTHUR, JAMES, FIRST EARL (1848-1930). Chief secretary for Ireland 1887-91; first lord of treasury 1891-2, 1895-1902; prime minister of Britain 1902-5; first lord of admiralty 1915-16; foreign secretary 1916-19; lord president of council 1919-22; created earl 1922.

BARTON, EDMUND (1849-1920). First prime minister of Australian Commonwealth 1901-3.

BESANT, ANNIE (1847-1933). Theosophist, educationist and politician; came to India 1893; president of Theosophical Society 1907-33; president of Indian National Congress 1917.

BIKANER, MAHARAJA OF (GANGA SINGH) (1880-1943). Succeeded 1887; assumed ruling powers 1898; chancellor of chamber of princes 1921-6.

BIRKENHEAD, FIRST EARL OF (F. E. SMITH) (1872-1930). Conservative M. P. 1906-18; attorney-general 1915-19; lord chancellor 1919-22; secretary of state for India 1924-8.

BORDEN, ROBERT (1854-1937). Statesman; prime minister of Canada 1911-20.

BOSE, SUBHAS CHANDRA (1897-1945). President of Indian National Congress 1938, 1939; escaped to Germany 1942; formed Indian National Army 1943.

BOTHA, LOUIS (1862-1919). Soldier and statesman; first prime minister of Union of South Africa 1910-19.

BRIGHT, JOHN (1811-89). Liberal statesman.

CAMPBELL-BANNERMAN, HENRY (1836-1908). Liberal M.P. 1868-1908; prime minister of Britain 1905-8.

CHAMBERLAIN, AUSTEN (1863-1937). Liberal Unionist M. P. 1892-1937; chancellor of exchequer 1903-5, 1919-21; secretary of state for India 1915-17; member of war cabinet 1918; foreign secretary 1924-9; first lord of admiralty 1931.

CHAMBERLAIN, JOSEPH (1836-1914). Statesman and social reformer; president of board of trade 1880-5; president of local government board 1886; resigned on introduction of Irish home rule bill 1886; colonial secretary 1895-1903.

CHELMSFORD, FIRST VISCOUNT (F.J.N. THESIGER) (1868-1933). Governor of Queensland 1905-9 and of New South Wales 1909-13; governor-general of India 1916-21; first lord of admiralty 1924.

CHURCHILL, WINSTON SPENCER (1874-1965). Under-secretary for colonies 1906-8; president of board of trade 1908-10; home secretary 1910-11; first lord of admiralty 1911-15, 1939-40; minister of munitions 1917; secretary of state for war 1919-21; colonial secretary 1921-2; chancellor of exchequer 1924-9; prime minister of Britain 1940-5, 1950-5.

COBDEN, RICHARD (1804-65). Statesman; a foremost leader of Anti-Corn Law League.

CONGREVE, RICHARD (1818-99). Positivist philosopher.

COTTON, HENRY JOHN STEDMAN (1845-1915). Entered Indian civil service 1867; chief commissioner of Assam 1896-1902; president of Indian National Congress 1904; Liberal M. P. 1906-10.

COUPLAND, REGINALD (1884-1952). Author and teacher.

COURTNEY, LEONARD HENRY, FIRST BARON (1832-1918). Journalist and statesman.

CREWE, MARQUESS OF (R.O.A. CREWE-MILNES) (1858-1945). Viceroy of Ireland 1892-5; lord president of council 1905-8, 1915-16; lord privy seal 1908-11, 1912-15; colonial secretary 1908-10; secretary of state for India 1910-15; president of board of education 1916; ambassador at Paris 1922-8; secretary of state for war 1931.

CROSS, RICHARD ASSHETON, FIRST VISCOUNT (1823-1914). Conservative politician; home secretary 1885-6; secretary of state for India 1886-92; lord privy seal 1895-1900.

CURTIS, LIONEL (1872-1955). A leading exponent of federalism; fellow of All Souls College, Oxford; one of the most influential 'backroom' figures of his day.

CURZON, GEORGE NATHANIEL, MARQUESS CURZON OF KEDLESTON (1859-1925). Under-secretary for India 1891-2; governor-general of India 1898-1905; lord president of council and member of war cabinet 1916-18; foreigne secretary 1919-24.

Biographical Notes

DILKE, CHARLES WENTWORTH (1843-1911). Author and politician.
DISRAELI, BENJAMIN, FIRST EARL OF BEACONSFIELD (1804-1881). Man of letters and statesman; prime minister of Britain 1868, 1874-80.
DUFFERIN, FIRST MARQUESS OF (1826-1902). Under-secretary for India 1864-6; governor-general of Canada 1872-8; ambassador at St. Petersburg 1879-81 and at Constantinople 1881-2; special commissioner to Egypt 1882-3; governor-general of India 1884-8; ambassador at Rome 1889-91 and at Paris 1891-6.
DUKE, WILLIAM (1863-1924). Entered Indian civil service 1882; lieutenant-governor of Bengal 1912-14; member of secretary of state's council 1914-20; permanent under-secretary of state, India Office 1920-4.
DYER, REGINALD EDWARD HARRY (1864-1927). Brigadier-general; responsible for Amritsar massacre 13 April 1919.
GANDHI, MOHANDAS KARAMCHAND (1869-1948). Called to bar 1889; went to South Africa 1893; returned to India 1915; leading figure of Indian National Congress till his assassination.
GHOSE, AUROBINDO (1872-1950). Passed written examination for Indian civil service but did not take riding test 1890; teacher at Baroda 1893-1906; leader of Bengali extremists 1906-10; retired to Pondicherry in 1910 and devoted himself to spiritualism.
GOKHALE, GOPAL KRISHNA (1866-1915). Teacher and journalist at Poona; member of Bombay legislative council 1899-1901 and of Indian legislative council 1901-15; president of Indian National Congress 1905.
HAMILTON, LORD GEORGE FRANCIS (1845-1927). Conservative politician; under-secretary for India 1874-80; first lord of admiralty 1885-6, 1886-92; secretary of state for India 1895-1903.
HARDINGE, CHARLES, BARON HARDINGE OF PENSHURST (1858-1944). Entered Foreign Office 1880; under-secretary of state 1903-4; ambassador at St. Petersburg 1904-6; permanent under-secretary of state 1906-10; governor-general of India 1910-16.
HARTINGTON, MARQUESS OF (SPENCER COMPTON CAVENDISH) (1833-1908). Chief secretary for Ireland 1870-4; secretary of state for India 1880-2; secretary of state for war 1882-5; lord president of council 1895-1903.
HERTZOG, JAMES BARRY MUNNIK (1866-1942). Prime minister of South Africa 1924-39.
HOLDERNESS, T.W. (1849-1929). Entered Indian civil service 1872; secretary, revenue and agriculture department, government of India 1898-1901; secretary, revenue, statistics and commerce department, India Office 1901-12; permanent under-secretary of state, India Office 1912-19; created baron 1920.
IRWIN, FIRST BARON (EDWARD FREDERICK LINDLEY WOOD), THIRD VISCOUNT AND FIRST EARL HALIFAX (1881-1959). Under-secretary for colonies 1921-2; president of board of education 1922-4; 1932-5; governor-general of India 1926-31; secretary of state for war 1935; lord privy seal 1935-7; foreign secretary 1938-40; ambassador at Washington 1941-6.

Biographical Notes

ISLINGTON, BARON (JOHN POYNDER DICKSON-POYNDER) (1866-1936). Governor of New Zealand 1910-12; chairman of royal commission on Indian public services 1912-14; under-secretary of state for colonies 1914-15 and for India 1915-18.

JANG, SALAR (1829-83). Prime minister of Hyderabad 1853-83.

JINNAH, MAHOMED ALI (1876-1948). Lawyer and politician; president of Muslim League 1916, 1920, and from 1934 until his death; governor-general of Pakistan 1947-8.

KERR, PHILIP (1882-1940). Member of Milner's 'Kindergarten'; editor of *Round Table* 1910-16; private secretary to Lloyd George 1916-21; succeeded to title as eleventh marquess of Lothian 1930; under-secretary of state for India 1931-2; ambassador at Washington 1939-40.

KISCH, C. H. (1884-1961). Entered India Office 1908; private secretary to permanent under-secretary 1911 and to parliamentary under-secretary in addition 1915; private secretary to secretary of state for India 1917-21; secretary, financial department 1921-33; assistant under-secretary 1933-43; deputy under-secretary 1943-6.

LANSDOWNE, FIFTH MARQUESS OF (HENRY CHARLES KEITH PETTY-FITZMAURICE) (1845-1927). Under-secretary for war 1872-4; under-secretary for India 1880; governor-general of Canada 1883-8; governor-general of India 1888-94; secretary of state for war 1895-1900; foreign secretary 1900-5.

LAURIER, WILFRID (1841-1919). Prime minister of Canada 1896-1911.

LLOYD GEORGE, DAVID (1863-1945). Liberal M.P. 1890-1945; president of board of trade 1905-9; chancellor of exchequer 1908-15; prime minister of Britain 1916-22; created earl 1945.

LONG, WALTER HUME, FIRST VISCOUNT (1854-1924). President of board of agriculture 1895-1900; president of local government board 1900-5, 1915-16; colonial secretary 1916-18; first lord of admiralty 1919-21; created viscount 1921.

LYALL, ALFRED COMYN (1835-1911). Entered Indian civil service 1856; lieutenant-governor of North-Western Provinces 1882-7; member of secretary of state's council 1887-1902.

LYTTELTON, ALFRED (1857-1913). Lawyer and statesman; colonial secretary 1903-5.

MACKAY, JAMES LYLE, FIRST EARL OF INCHAPE (1852-1932). Chairman and director of numerous banking and shipping concerns; member of council of secretary of state for India 1897-1911.

MARRIS, WILLIAM, (1874-1945). Entered Indian civil service 1896; seconded to Transvaal government 1906-8; joint secretary in home department, government of India 1917-18; governor of Assam 1921-2 and of United Provinces 1922-7; member of secretary of state's council 1927-9.

MAYO, SIXTH EARL OF (RICHARD SOUTHWELL BOURKE) (1822-72). Chief secretary for Ireland 1852-69; governor-general of India 1869-72.

MEHTA, PHEROZESHAH M. (1845-1915). Lawyer and politician; member of Bombay legislative council 1887-9, 1893-4 and of Indian legisla-

Biographical Notes

tive council 1894-6, 1898-1901; president of Indian National Congress 1890.

MERRIMAN, JOHN XAVIER (1841-1926). South African statesman; prime minister of Cape Colony 1908-10.

MESTON, JAMES SCORGIE, FIRST BARON (1865-1943). Entered Indian civil service 1885; lieutenant-governor of United Provinces 1912-18; finance member of governor-general's council 1918-19; created baron 1919.

MILNER, ALFRED, VISCOUNT (1854-1925). Director-general of accounts, Egypt 1889; under-secretary for finance, Egypt 1890-2; high commissioner for South Africa 1897-1905; created viscount 1902; member of Lloyd George's war cabinet 1916-18; secretary of state for war 1918; colonial secretary 1918-21.

MINTO, FOURTH EARL OF (GILBERT JOHN MURRAY KYNYMOND ELLIOTT) (1845-1914). Governor-general of Canada 1898-1904; governor-general of India 1905-10.

MONTAGU, EDWIN SAMUEL (1879-1924). Liberal M.P. 1906-22; under-secretary for India 1910-14; financial secretary to treasury 1914-16; chancellor of Duchy of Lancaster 1915; minister of munitions 1916; resigned December 1916; secretary of state for India 1917-22.

MORLEY, JOHN, VISCOUNT (1838-1923). Man of letters and statesman; chief secretary for Ireland 1886, 1892-5; secretary of state for India 1905-10; created viscount 1908.

MOUNTBATTEN OF BURMA, FIRST EARL (LOUIS FRANCIS ALBERT VICTOR NICHOLAS MOUNTBATTEN) (1900-   ). Chief of combined operations 1942-3; supreme Allied commander South-East Asia 1943-6; governor-general of India 1947-8.

NAOROJI, DADABHAI (1825-1917). Businessman, journalist and politician; first Indian member of British Parliament 1892-5; president of Indian National Congress 1886, 1893, 1906.

NEHRU, JAWAHARLAL (1889-1964). Man of letters and statesman; president of Indian National Congress 1929, 1936, 1937, 1946, 1951-4; prime minister of India 1947-64.

NORTHBROOK, FIRST EARL OF (THOMAS GEORGE BARING) (1826-1904). Under-secretary at India Office 1859-64, at War Office 1861, 1868, at Home Office 1864; secretary to admiralty 1866; governor-general of India 1872-6; first lord of admiralty 1880-4; special commissioner to Egypt 1884.

PAL, BIPIN CHANDRA (1858-1932). Author and journalist.

POLLOCK, FREDERICK (1845-1937). Jurist.

RAO, MADHAVA (1828-91). Prime minister of Travancore 1858-72, of Indore 1873-5 and of Baroda 1875-82.

RAU, B.N. (1887-1953). Indian civil servant and jurist.

RIPON, FIRST MARQUESS OF (GEORGE FREDERICK SAMUEL ROBINSON) (1827-1909). Secretary of state for India 1866; governor-general of India 1880-4; colonial secretary 1892-5; lord privy seal 1905-8.

RISLEY, HERBERT (1851-1911). Entered Indian civil service 1873; secretary in home department, government of India 1902-9; member of governor-general's council 1909-10; secretary in judicial and public department, India Office 1910-11.

ROBERTS, CHARLES (1865-1959). Liberal M. P. 1906-8, 1922-3; under-secretary of state for India 1914-15.

ROSEBERY, FIFTH EARL OF (ARCHIBALD PHILIP PRIMROSE) (1847-1929). Author and statesmen; secretary of state for foreign affairs 1886, 1892-4; prime minister of Britain 1894-5.

SALISBURY, THIRD MARQUESS OF (ROBERT ARTHUR TALBOT GASCOYNE-CECIL) (1830-1903). Conservative politician; secretary of state for India 1866-7, 1874-8; prime minister of Britain 1885, 1886-92, 1895-1902.

SETON, M.C. (1872-1940). Entered India Office 1898; secretary, judicial and public department 1911-19; assistant under-secretary 1919; deputy under-secretary 1924-33.

SHAFI, MUHAMMAD (1869-1932). Lawyer and politician; president of Muslim League 1913, 1927; member of governor-general's council 1919-24.

SCHUCKBURGH, J.E. (1877-1953). Entered India Office 1900; assistant secretary, political department 1912-17; secretary 1917-21; transferred to Colonial Office 1921; assistant under-secretary 1921-31; deputy under-secretary 1931-42.

SINHA, SATYENDRA PRASANNA (1864-1928). Advocate-general of Bengal 1905-9; law member of governor-general's council 1909-10; president of Indian National Congress 1915; created baron 1919; under-secretary of state for India 1919-20; governor of Bihar and Orissa 1920-1; member of judicial committee of privy council 1926-8.

SMITH, SAMUEL (1836-1906). Businessman, philanthropist and politician; Liberal M.P. 1882-1905.

SMUTS, JAN CHRISTIAN (1870-1950). Statesman; prime minister of South Africa 1919-24.

TILAK, BAL GANGADHAR (1856-1920). Teacher and journalist at Poona; jailed for sedition 1897-8, 1908-14.

WEDGWOOD, JOSIAH CLEMENT, FIRST BARON (1872-1943). M.P. 1906-42; left Liberal for Labour party 1919; chancellor of Duchy of Lancaster 1924; created baron 1942.

WILLINGDON, FIRST MARQUESS OF (FREEMAN FREEMAN-THOMAS) (1866-1941). Liberal M.P. 1900-10; governor of Bombay 1913-18, of Madras 1919-24; governor-general of Canada 1926-30; governor-general of India 1931-6.

NOTES

CHAPTER 1

[1] In 1891, however, G.B. Barton noted 'a decided tendency of the present time to revive it [the term "Commonwealth"]'. See his *The Draft Bill to Constitute the Commonwealth of Australia* (Sydney, 1891), p. 11.

[2] For example, at the Australian National Conventions of 1891 and 1897, objections were raised to the proposed title of 'Commonwealth' for the federation of Australia mainly on the ground that it was suggestive of republicanism. See *Official Record of the Proceedings and Debates of the National Australasian Convention, Sydney, March-April 1891* (Sydney, 1891), pp. 266-9; and *Official Report of the National Australasian Convention, Adelaide, March 22 to May 5, 1897* (Adelaide, 1897), pp. 616-18. In 1900 Queen Victoria had similar misgivings about the title and Joseph Chamberlain had to assure her that 'there was no anti-monarchical intention'. See J. Chamberlain to Lord Salisbury, 22 January 1900, Salisbury Papers, Christ Church, Oxford.

[3] 'Commonwealth' and 'Commonweal' were, in fact, at one time used as interchangeable words in sense 2. See, for example, Richard Hooker, *Of the Laws of Ecclesiastical Polity* (London, 1953-7), and Edward Forset, *A Comparative Discourse of the Bodies Natural and Politique* (London, 1606). See also on this point an illuminating article by Professor W. K. Hancock, 'A Veray and True Comyn Wele', *Australian Rhodes Review*, March 1934, pp. 20-32.

[4] Marquess of Crewe, *Lord Rosebery* (London, 1931), vol. i, p. 186.

[5] The idea of a commonwealth of nations, which was, in fact, an extension of the mediaeval idea of a commonwealth of Christendom, has been traced back to Francisco de Vitoria (1480-1546) and Francisco Suarez (1548-1617), the Spanish writers on international law. [See James Brown Scott, *The Spanish Conception of International Law and Sanctions* (Washington, 1934).] It was, however, more definitely formulated by the German writer Christian de Wolff (1679-1754) in his *Jus Gentium Methodo Scientifica Pertractatum* (1749; English translation by Joseph H. Drake, Oxford, 1934). Wolff argued that nature herself had established a commonwealth among all nations for their welfare, and that as individuals were bound to submit to the laws of the particular commonwealth of which they were members, in the same way, it was the duty of nations to submit to the rules of the commonwealth of nations of which they were all members. The Latin phrase *civitas gentium maxima*, used by Wolff, was variously translated into English

as 'the (great) commonwealth of nations', 'the commonwealth of states', 'the universal commonwealth', 'the republic of nations', 'the society of nations', 'the family of nations', 'the international community', 'the federation of states', etc. For the use of the phrase 'commonwealth of nations' see James Wilson, *Lectures on Law, Delivered in the College of Philadelphia, in the Years 1790 and 1791, Works* (Philadelphia, 1804), vol. i, pp. 45, 226, 359; Henry Wheaton, *History of the Law of Nations* (New York, 1845), p. 178, *Elements of International Law* (ed. A. C. Boyd, London, 1878), p. 10; R. Phillimore, *Commentaries upon International Law* (London, 1854), vol. i, pp. 7, 88; T. D. Woolsey, *Introduction to the Study of International Law* (Boston, 1860), pp. 68-9; T. Twiss, *The Law of Nations* (Oxford, 1861), vol. i, p. 113; Sir E. Creasy, *First Platform of International Law* (London, 1876), pp. vii, 48, 102, 285, 431, 681. See also E. Burke, *Letters on the Proposals for Peace with the Regicide Directory of France* (London, 1796), *Works* (London, 1823), vol. viii, p. 109; and T.B. Macaulay, *The History of England from the Accession of James II* (London, 1849-55), vol. i, p. 230; vol. iii, p. 14; vol. iv, p. 257.

[6] Rosebery, *Questions of Empire* (London, 1900), p. 6.

[7] See, for example, Rosebery, *The Union of England and Scotland* (London, 1871), p. 30; *Appreciations and Addresses Delivered by Lord Rosebery* (ed. Charles Geake, London, 1899), pp. 192, 235; and his letter to the City Liberal Club, published in *The Times*, 17 July 1901.

[8] Rosebery, *Questions of Empire*, pp. 13, 24, 35.

[9] N. Mansergh, *The Name and Nature of the British Commonwealth* (London, 1954), p. 2.

[10] Lord Blachford, 'The Integrity of the British Empire', *Nineteenth Century*, October 1877, p. 361.

[11] Goldwin Smith, 'The Greatness of England', *Contemporary Review*, December 1878, p. 17. See also his 'Straining the Silken Thread', *Macmillan's Magazine*, August 1888, p. 244; *Canada and the Canadian Question* (London, 1891), p. 239; *Essays on Questions of the Day* (New York, 1893), p. 127; *The United Kingdom: A Political History* (London, 1899), vol. ii, pp. 384-5.

[12] J. R. Seeley, *The Expansion of England* (London, 1883), p. 37.

[13] Bernard Shaw, *Fabianism and the Empire* (London, 1900), pp. 49-50.

[14] Sir Perceval Laurence, *The Life of John Xavier Merriman* (London, 1930), pp. 230, 370.

[15] See, for example, his article, entitled 'The Closer Union of the Empire', in *Nineteenth Century*, April 1887, pp. 508, 511, 512, and his speech in the Cape House of Assembly on 11 September 1902, *The Case against the Suspension of the Constitution of Cape Colony* (Capetown, 1902), p. 12.

[16] *The Times*, 30 October 1905. The correspondence between Merriman and the secretary of the British Empire League, Freeman Murray, was published in *The Times* of 30 October 1905, which also commented on it in a leading article. See also *British Empire Review*, November 1905, pp. 84-6, and February 1906, pp. 132-3.

[17] Thomas MacFarlane, a Canadian imperial federationist, used the phrases 'British Commonwealth', 'Imperial Commonwealth' and 'Anglo-Saxon Commonwealth' in his *Within the Empire* (Ottawa, 1891). The follow-

Notes

ing remark by Guilford L. Molesworth ('Imperialism for India', *Calcutta Review*, June 1885, pp. 269-70) would suggest that the word 'Commonwealth' was being used as a name for the ideal of a united Empire before 1885: 'If India is to be saved it must be by the strong effort of a wide, comprehensive policy, which will knit it, with our Colonies into one mighty federation ... whether it be under the name of "United States", "United Kingdom", "Commonwealth", "Empire" or "Greater Britain".' See also J. A. Froude, *Oceana; or England and her Colonies* (London, 1886), *passim;* and the remark made by J. Ballance on 3 August 1891 in the New Zealand Parliament, *New Zealand Parliamentary Debates*, 1891, vol. lxxiii, p. 69.

[18] J. Chamberlain, *Foreign and Colonial Speeches* (London, 1897), p. 248.
[19] *Edinburgh Review*, July 1900, p. 252.
[20] 'Our Lady of the Snow', *Rudyard Kipling's Verse* (London, 1940), pp. 182-4.
[21] 'The Young Queen', *ibid.*, pp. 187-8.
[22] C. Headlam (ed.), *The Milner Papers* (London, 1933), vol. ii, p. 287.
[23] A. Milner, *The Nation and the Empire* (London, 1913), p. 90.
[24] R. Jebb, 'Colonial Nationalism', *Empire Review*, August 1902, pp. 6-15, and *Studies in Colonial Nationalism* (London, 1905).
[25] Cited in J. S. Ewart, *The Kingdom Papers* (Ottawa, 1912), vol. i, p. 8. See also J. Chamberlain's speech at Birmingham on 27 June 1905, in C. W. Boyd (ed.), *Mr. Chamberlain's Speeches* (London, 1914), vol. ii, p. 328.
[26] Curzon, *The True Imperialism* (Birmingham, 1907), p. 20.
[27] Milner, 'Some Reflections on the Coming Conference', *National Review*, April 1907, p. 195.
[28] *Ibid.* [29] *Ibid.*, pp. 195-6.
[30] Milner, 'The Meaning of Wider Patriotism', *Standard of Empire*, 23 May 1908.
[31] Milner, 'The Two Empires', *Proceedings of the Royal Colonial Institute*, 1907-8, vol. xxxix, pp. 329-30.
[32] *Ibid.*, p. 330. [33] *Ibid.*
[34] W. M. Childs, 'Towards an Imperial Policy', *National Review*, October 1908, p. 216.
[35] Froude, *Oceana; or England and her Colonies* p. 12.
[36] M. H. Hervey, 'The Latest Phase of Imperial Federation', *Imperial and Asiatic Quarterly Review*, January 1891, p. 142. See also his 'Lord Carrington upon "Australia as I saw it" ', *United Services Magazine*, March 1891, p. 544.
[37] Arnold White, 'Britannia and the Colonist', *National Review*, June 1900, p. 640.
[38] *Ibid.*
[39] J. S. Ewart, *The Kingdom of Canada* (Toronto, 1908), p. 6. See also his *The Kingdom Papers* (Ottawa, 1912), vol. i, p. 2.
[40] New Zealand (120), *Round Table Studies, First Series, Annotated (Green) Memorandum on Canada* (privately circulated, London, 1911), p. 395.
[41] *Ibid.*
[42] *United Empire*, August 1911, p. 540.
[43] Curzon, *op. cit.*, p. 10.

⁴⁴Cited in Richard Jebb, *Studies in Colonial Nationalism*, p. 1.
⁴⁵*Minutes of Proceedings of the Imperial Conference, 1911*, Cd. 5745, p. 98.
⁴⁶*The Times*, 3 May 1900.
⁴⁷The phrase is Sir Henry Campbell-Bannerman's. See J. A. Spender, *The Life of the Right Hon. Sir Henry Campbell-Bannerman* (London, 1923), vol. i, p. 336, vol. ii, p. 9.
⁴⁸See J.A. Hobson's powerful book, *Imperialism: A Study* (London, 1902).
⁴⁹Rosebery in his letter to the City Liberal Club, *The Times*, 17 July 1901.
⁵⁰See, for example, Lord Carnarvon, 'Imperial Administration', *Fortnightly Review*, 1 December 1878, pp. 751-64; T. H. S. Escott, *Pillars of the Empire* (London, 1879), p. xxx; and R. Seeley, *The Expansion of England*, pp. 31, 73.
⁵¹Bernard Shaw, *op. cit.*, p. 88.
⁵²Henry Newbolt, 'The Paradox of Imperialism', *Monthly Review*, October 1900, p. 9.
⁵³Rosebery, *Questions of Empire*, p. 6. See also A. W. Jose, *The Growth of the Empire* (London, 1901), p. 1; F.S. Oliver, 'From Empire to Union', *National Review*, March 1909, Special Supplement, p. 1-36; C. P. Lucas, *Greater Rome and Greater Britain* (Oxford, 1912), p. 8.
⁵⁴Milner, *The Nation and the Empire*, p. 90.
⁵⁵J. S. Little, *Progress of the British Empire in the Century* (London, 1903), p. 100.
⁵⁶See *Monthly Review*, October 1900, pp. 1-14; November 1900, pp. 1-10; January 1901, pp. 10-19; March 1901, pp. 1-9; October 1902, pp. 1-5; November 1902, pp. 1-9; June 1903, pp. 1-10.
⁵⁷See, for example, F. S. Oliver, 'From Empire to Union', *National Review*, March 1909, Special Supplement, pp. 1-36.
⁵⁸See also his address before the Royal Society of Arts on 1 February 1910, 'Imperial Colonial Development: A New Doctrine for a British Commonwealth', *Journal of the Royal Society of Arts*, 18 February 1910, vol. lviii, pp. 333-49.
⁵⁹*Round Table Studies, Second Series, Instalment A* (London, 1912). See also *Round Table Studies, Second Series, Instalment B* (London, 1913), *Instalment C* (London, 1914), and *Instalment D* (London, 1914); *The Round Table Movement, Its Past and Its Future* (London, 1913); *A Practical Enquiry into the Nature of Citizenship in the British Empire and into the Relations of Its Several Communities to Each Other* (London, 1914); *The Problem of the Commonwealth* (London, 1915); *The Project of a Commonwealth* (London, 1915); *The Problem of the Commonwealth* (London, 1916); and *The Commonwealth of Nations* (London, 1916). All but the last two of these works were printed for private circulation only.

In an account which he later gave to Professor W. K. Hancock [see Hancock, *Survey of British Commonwealth Affairs*, vol. i, *Problems of Nationality* (Oxford, 1937), p. 54], Curtis did not say precisely in what year he began using the term 'Commonwealth', to describe the British Empire. The term does not appear in Curtis's writings before 1912 [see the so-called *Green Memoranda* on Canada, Australia, and New Zealand (1910-11), and *The Form of an Organic Union of the Empire* (London, 1911)]. It appears for the first time in the *Round Table Studies, Second Series, Instalment A* (London, 1912). [Suprisingly enough, the term 'Commonwealth' does not appear in any form in the *Round Table* quarterly until March 1914, pp. 229, 276, 277, 279.] Though Curtis frequently used the terms 'Commonwealth', 'British Commonwealth' and 'Imperial Commonwealth', to describe the British Empire during 1912-15, he does not seem to have used the phrase 'Commonwealth of Nations' until 1916. That particular phrase appears only in the title of the book, *The Commonwealth of Nations* (London, 1916), and not in the text. The book was first printed for private circulation in 1915 under the title of *The Project of a Commonwealth*. When it was published for the general public in the spring of 1916, its title was 'changed to The Commonwealth of Nations' in order 'to avoid confusion with the smaller volume', *The Problem of the Commonwealth,* published almost simultaneously [see Curtis's Preface (April 1916) to *The Commonwealth of Nations* (1916)]. The phrase 'Commonwealth of Nations' does not occur in the *Round Table* quarterly until June 1917, pp. 455-8.

[60]R. Jebb, *The Britannic Question* (London, 1913), pp. 15, 16, 24, 80, 81, 142, 180, 252, 253; 'The Ideal Empire of Our Time', *Britannic Review*, May 1914, 31-45.

[61]See *Britannic Review* (ed. Ben H. Morgan), May 1914, pp. 1-30; June 1914, pp. 145-70; July 1914, pp. 275-95; August 1914, pp. 401-38.

[62]Philip H. Kerr, 'Commonwealth and Empire', *The Empire and the Future* (ed. A. P. Newton, London, 1916), pp. 73-4.

[63]*Ibid.*

[64]Included in *The War and Democracy* (ed. A. E. Zimmern, London, 1914), ch. ix, pp. 348-74.

[65]*Ibid.*, pp. 379-81.

[66]See, for example, A.E. Zimmern, *The War and Democracy* (London, 1914,) *passim*, and *Nationality and Government* (London, 1918), *passim;* J.A. Hobson, *Towards International Government* (London, 1915), p. 212; E.D. Morel, *Truth and the War* (London, 1916), pp. 184-5, 187; L. Curtis, *The Problem of the Commonwealth* (London, 1916), *passim*, and *The Commonwealth of Nations* (London, 1916), *passim;* A. P. Newton (ed.), *The Empire and the Future* (London, 1916), *passim;* J. C. Smuts, *Wartime Speeches* (London, 1917), *passim;* A. F. Pollard, *The Commonwealth at War* (London, 1917), *passim;* V. H. Rutherford, *Commonwealth or Empire?* (London, 1917), *passim.*

[67]*Imperial War Conference, 1917. Extracts from Minutes of Proceedings and Papers Laid before the Conference*, Cd. 8566 (1917), p. 41.

[68]*Ibid.*, p. 47.   [69]*Ibid.*, pp. 5, 61.

[70]J. C. Smuts, *Wartime Speeches* (London, 1917), p. 31.

[71]*Ibid.*, p. 32. For a slightly different text see Smuts, *The British Commonwealth of Nations* (London, 1917), p. 5.

[72]A. E. Zimmern, *The War and Democracy*, pp. 370-1: 'So wrote Lord Acton ... fifty years ago, when the watchwords of Nationality were on all

men's lips, adding, in words that were prophetic of the failure of the Austrian and the progress of the British Commonwealth of Nations . . . .'

[73] *Imperial War Conference, 1918. Extracts from Minutes of Proceedings and Papers Laid before the Conference*, Cd. 9177 (1918), p. 18.
[74] *Ibid.*, p. 15.
[75] *Ibid.*, p. 65.
[76] Cited in H. Duncan Hall, 'The Genesis of the Balfour Declaration of 1926', *Journal of Commonwealth Political Studies*, November 1962, p. 177.
[77] See A.B. Keith, *Speeches and Documents on the British Dominions, 1918-31* (Oxford, 1948), p. 77.
[78] *Imperial Conference, 1926. Summary of Proceedings*, Cmd. 2786 (1926), p. 77.
[79] See A.B. Keith, *op. cit.*, p. 303.
[80] W. K. Hancock, *Survey of British Commonwealth Affairs*, vol. i, *Problems of Nationality*, p. 58.
[81] *Official Report of the National Australian Convention, Adelaide, March 22 to May 5, 1897*, p. 618.

CHAPTER 2

[1] Sir Frederick Whyte, *India: A Bird's-Eye View* (London, 1943), p. 13.
[2] *Ibid.*
[3] *Minutes of the Proceedings of the Colonial Conference, 1907*, Cd. 3523 (1907), pp. 78-94.
[4] A. Milner, 'The Two Empires', *Proceedings of the Royal Colonial Institute*, 1907-8, vol. xxxix, pp. 329-37; also *The Nation and the Empire* (London, 1913), pp. 289-300.
[5] This classification became popular with a group of thinkers on imperial problems. See, for example, an article entitled 'The Two Empires' in *The Times*, 24 May 1909, and a chapter with the heading 'The Two Empires' in C. P. Lucas, *Greater Rome and Greater Britain* (Oxford, 1912), pp. 131-55.
[6] Milner, *The Nation and the Empire*, p. 290.
[7] 'Reproduction is the key-note of the sphere of settlement, government is the key-note of the sphere of rule.' C. P. Lucas, *Greater Rome and Greater Britain*, p. 142.
[8] C.W. Dilke, *Greater Britain* (London, 1868), 2 vols.
[9] Lucas, *op. cit.*, p. 142.
[10] A.J. Toynbee, *The Conduct of British Empire Foreign Relations since the Peace Settlement* (Oxford, 1928), p. 37.
[11] Percival Spear has the following interesting thought: 'The same doctrine of the supremacy of Parliament which was about to lose the Thirteen Colonies to Britain was to prove the instrument for transferring Anglo-Saxon values and institutions to the Indian subcontinent.' *India: A Modern History* (Ann Arbor, 1972), p. 210.
[12] E. Barker, *Ideas and Ideals of the British Empire* (Cambridge, 1941), pp. 12-23. J. R. Seeley regarded the British Empire in India as 'Oriental' and

the British government therein an 'un-English'. *The Expansion of England* (London, 1883), pp. 190, 302, 304.

[13]'British authority in India may be traced, historically, to a twofold source. It is derived partly from the British Crown and Parliament, partly from the Great Mogul and other native rulers of India.' C.P. Ilbert, *The Government of India* (Oxford, 1898), p. 1.

[14]'Of the sphere of rule it may be said that the English are in it but not of it; of the sphere of settlement that the English are both in it and of it....' Lucas, *op. cit.*, p. 142.

[15]'Carrying their nationality with them, they claimed everywhere the rights of Englishmen.' Seeley, *op. cit.*, p. 67.

[16]G.C. Lewis, *An Essay on the Government of Dependencies* (Oxford, 1891 ed.), pp. 159-60.

[17]C.B. Adderley, *Review of 'The Colonial Policy of Lord John Russell's Administration', by Earl Grey, 1853; and of Subsequent Colonial History* (London, 1869), p. 14.

[18]C.P. Lucas, 'British Colonial Administration and its Agencies', in A.J. Herbertson and O.J.R. Howarth (eds.), *The Oxford Survey of the British Empire* (Oxford, 1914), vol. vi, p. 24.

[19]O. M. Dickerson, *American Colonial Government 1696-1765* (Cleveland, 1912), p. 173; also quoted in J. H. Rose and others (eds.), *The Cambridge History of the British Empire* (Cambridge, 1929), vol. i, p. 616.

[20]*The Cambridge History of the British Empire*, vol. i, p. 409.

[21]*The Oxford Survey of the British Empire*, vol. vi, p. 24.

[22]H.H. Dodwell (ed.), *The Cambridge History of India* (Delhi, 1963 reprint), vol. v, p. 181; C. H. Philips, *The East India Company 1784-1834* (Manchester, 1940), pp. 32-4.

[23]*Parliamentary History*, vol. xxii (1781-2), col. 1285.

[24]*The Oxford Survey of the British Empire*, vol. vi, p. 5.

[25]*Ibid.*

[26]The term 'Anglo-Indians' is used here in its original sense of British persons residing or having resided in India.

[27]*Report on Indian Constitutional Reforms*, Cd. 9109 (1918), p. 29.

[28]*Ibid.*, p. 30.

[29]See C. A. Bodelsen, *Studies in Mid-Victorian Imperialism* (Copenhagen, 1924), pp. 32-59.

[30]'Even the anti-imperialists who foresaw the rapid disintegration of the colonial system supposed that Indians would not be capable of self-government for generations yet.' C. E. Carrington, *The British Overseas* (Cambridge, 1950), p. 940.

[31]R. Congreve, *India* (London, 1857), pp. 44-6; also 'India', in *Essays: Political, Social, and Religious* (London, 1874), pp. 76-7.

[32]J.E. Thorold Rogers (ed.), *Public Addresses by John Bright, M.P.* (London, 1879), pp. 448, 502.

[33]G. Smith, *The Empire* (Oxford, 1863), pp. 8, 257, 292.

[34]Paul Boell, *L'Inde et le Probleme Indien*, p. 289, cited in Lord Cromer, *Ancient and Modern Imperialism* (London, 1910), p. 124. John Morley told the House of Commons on 6 June 1907: 'There is, I know, a school... who

say that we might wisely walk out of India and leave it, and that the Indians would manage their own affairs better than we can manage them for them. I think anybody who pictures to himself the anarchy, the bloody chaos that would follow from any such deplorable step might shrink from any such decision.' *Parliamentary Debates*, vol. cixxv (1907), col. 886. See also his *Indian Speeches* (London, 1907), p. 33, for similar sentiments.

[35]See R. Coupland, *India: A Re-Statement* (Oxford, 1945), pp. 291-2.

[36]J.R. Seeley observed in the early 1880s that 'the abandonment of India is an idea which even those who believe that we shall one day be driven to it are not accustomed to contemplate as a practical scheme. ... A time may conceivably come when it may be practicable to leave India to herself, but for the present it is necessary to govern her as if we were to govern her for ever.' *The Expansion of England*, pp. 193-4.

[37]Lord Curzon shocked the peers by his outspokenness when he remarked in the House of Lords on 21 May 1908 that Indian tariffs were decided more 'by English than by purely Indian considerations' and added, 'I think it would be true, therefore, to say that the fiscal policy of India during the last thirty or forty years has been shaped far more in Manchester than in Calcutta.' *Parliamentary Debates*, vol. clxxxix (1908), coll. 436-7. Lord Morley 'felt a shiver' and Lord Rosebery remarked in real wrath, 'That's about the most dangerous thing I ever heard said in this House.' Morley to Minto, 22 May 1908, Morley Papers, India Office Library, London. E.S. Montagu told the Indian civilian William Marris, who urged fiscal autonomy for India, in November 1917 that 'this fear that self-government for India should lead to customs liberty was at the root of the Conservative opposition' to his appointment as secretary of state for India and that 'it would jeopardise any chance of getting any statute through the Houses of Parliament or through the Cabinet'. E.S. Montagu, *An Indian Diary* (London, 1930), p. 31.

[38]J. Coatman, *Years of Destiny: India 1926-1932* (London, 1932), p. 24.

[39]*Parliamentary History*, vol. xxiv (1783-5), col. 408.

[40]R. Coupland, *Britain and India 1600-1947* (London, 1948), pp. 19-20.

[41]E.M. Winslow, *The Pattern of Imperialism* (New York, 1948), pp. 11-12.

[42]Burke in the House of Commons on 1 December 1783. *Parliamentary History*, vol. xxiii (1782-3), coll. 1316-17.

[43]Lord Hailey, *The Position of Colonies in a British Commonwealth of Nations* (Oxford, 1941), pp. 10-11.

[44]*Parliamentary History*, vol. xxiv (1783-5), col. 1086.

[45]*Parliamentary Debates*, vol. xxv (1813), coll. 714-15; also quoted in H. H. Dodwell (ed.), *The Cambridge History of India* (Cambridge, 1932), vol. vi, pp. 1-2.

[46]The Charter Act of 1833 (3 & 4 Will. 4, c. 85) laid down that no native of India 'shall by reason only of his religion, place of birth, descent, colour, or any of them be disabled from holding any Place, Office, or Employment' under the East India Company. For the full text see R. Muir (ed.), *The*

Making of British India 1756-1858 (Manchester, 1915), p. 304.

[47] Barker, *op. cit.*, p. 54.

[48] C.P. Lucas, 'Empire and Democracy', in *The Empire and the Future* (London, 1916), p. 18.

[49] Quoted in *Report on Indian Constitutional Reforms*, Cd. 9109 (1918), p. 57.

[50] L. Wolf, *Life of the First Marquess of Ripon* (London, 1921), vol. ii, p. 100.

[51] See S.R. Mehrotra, *India and the Commonwealth 1885-1929* (London, 1965), p. 49.

[52] Morley to Minto, 1 June 1906, Morley Papers.

[53] Quoted in Cromer, *op. cit.*, p. 126.

[54] Minto to Morley, 28 May 1908, Morley Papers.

[55] Morley to Minto, 19 September 1907, *ibid.*

[56] Morley to Minto, 23 April 1908, *ibid.*

[57] Morley to Minto, 21 October 1909, *ibid.*

[58] 6 March 1947; 434 H.C. Deb. 5s., col. 678. Debate on prime minister Attlee's announcement, on 20 February 1947, of the 'definite intention' of the British government 'to take the necessary steps to effect the transference of power into responsible Indian hands by a date not later than June 1948'.

[59] See Mehrotra, *op. cit.*, pp. 86-7.

[60] Morley to Minto, 2 August 1906, Morley Papers.

[61] G.K. Gokhale, *Speeches of Gopal Krishna Gokhale* (Madras, 1920), p. 950.

[62] *Ibid.*, p. 949.

[63] Morley wrote to Minto on 8 October 1907: 'Force is all very well, and you cannot carry on government without it—open or reserved—either in India or anywhere else. But we British at any rate, cannot afford not to cultivate at the same time some sort of progressive elements.' On 31 October 1907 he again wrote to Minto that his ambition was to impress 'the ideal of "Order *plus* Progress" upon a great body of men here, who have been used to regard India with aversion, or indifference, or else with one of the two stupid ideas, that we have nothing to do but to keep the sword sharp, or on the other hand ... concede One Man One Vote'. Morley to Minto, 8, 31 October 1907, Morley Papers.

[64] Cd. 9109 (1918), p. 119.

[65] *Ibid.*, p. 148.

[66] 'It comes as rather a shock to us in these days to read some of our imperialist literature in the past and see how perilously near some of us have been to preaching the Prussian brand of imperialism.' Philip H. Kerr (later Lord Lothian), 'Commonwealth and Empire', in *The Empire and the Future*, pp. 73-4.

[67] 97 H. C. Deb. 5s., coll. 1695-6.

[68] A.E. Zimmern, *The Third British Empire* (Oxford, 1927), p. 3.

[69] *The Works of the Right Honourable Edmund Burke* (London, 1826), vol. xiii, p. 154. Opening speech in the impeachment of Warren Hastings.

[70] Zimmern, *op. cit.*, pp. 13-14.

CHAPTER 3

[1] C.A. Bodelsen, *Studies in Mid-Victorian Imperalism* (Copenhagen, 1924), p. 168.
[2] C.B. Adderley, *Review of 'The Colonial Policy of Lord John Russell's Administration', by Earl Grey, 1853, and of Subsequent Colonial History* (London, 1869), p. 3.
[3] W. F. Monypenny and G.E. Buckle, *The Life of Benjamin Disraeli, Earl of Beaconsfield* (London, 1910-20), vol. iii, p. 385.
[4] *Ibid.*, vol. iv, p. 476.
[5] J. Morley, *The Life of Richard Cobden* (London, 1881), vol. ii, pp. 470-1.
[6] G. Smith, *The Empire* (Oxford, 1863), p. 257.
[7] *Parliamentary History*, vol. xii (1781-2), col. 1285.
[8] G.C. Lewis, *An Essay on the Government of Dependencies* (Oxford, 1891 ed.), p .289.
[9] G. Smith, 'The Empire', *Essays on Questions of the Day* (New York, 1893,) p. 127.
[10] See P. E. Roberts, *India under Wellesley* (London, 1929), pp. 109, 136.
[11] R. Cobden, *How Wars Are Got Up in India* (London, 1853), p. 59.
[12] G. W. Dilke, *Greater Britain* (London, 1868), vol. ii, p. 394.
[13] G. Smith, *The Empire*, p. 292.
[14] Morley, *op. cit.*, pp. 206, 208.
[15] Cobden, *op. cit.*, p. 58.
[16] Morley, *op. cit.*, p. 205.   [17] *Ibid.*
[18] Cobden, *op. cit.*, p. 58.
[19] Morley, *op. cit.*, p. 210.
[20] *Ibid.*, pp. 206, 213-14, 216.
[21] *Ibid.*, pp. 206, 207, 208, 213.   [22] *Ibid.*, p. 212.
[23] *Ibid.*, pp. 208, 209, 210, 213.
[24] *Ibid.*, pp. 207, 210, 210.
[25] *Ibid.*, p. 210.   [26] *Ibid.*, p. 216.   [27] *Ibid.*, p. 213.
[28] *Ibid.*, p. 208.   [29] *Ibid.*, p. 206.
[30] Cobden, *op. cit.*, pp. 56, 58.
[31] Morley, *op. cit.*, p. 214.
[32] *Ibid.*, p. 213.   [33] *Ibid.*, p. 217.   [34] *Ibid.*
[35] E. Burke, *Works* (London, 1826-7), vol. iv, p. 44.
[36] J.E. Thorold Rogers (ed.), *Public Addresses by John Bright, M.P.* (London, 1879), p. 448.
[37] J.E. Thorold Rogers (ed.), *Speeches on Questions of Public Policy by the Right Honourable John Bright, M.P.* (London, 1890), p. 19.
[38] *Ibid.*, pp. 1-32.   [39] *Ibid.*, p. 19.   [40] *Ibid.*, p. 28.
[41] *Ibid.*   [42] *Ibid.*, p. 29.   [43] *Ibid.*, p. 32.
[44] *Ibid.*, p. 30.   [45] *Ibid.*, p. 31.   [46] *Ibid.*, pp. 31-2.
[47] See J. L. Sturgis, *John Bright and the Empire* (London, 1969), pp. 67-8.
[48] J. E. Thorold Rogers (ed.), *Public Addresses by John Bright, M.P.*, pp. 448, 502-3.
[49] *Ibid.*, p. 448.

Notes

⁵⁰R. Congreve, 'India', *Essays: Political, Social, and Religious* (London, 1874), p. 72.
⁵¹*Ibid.* ⁵²*Ibid.*, p. 76. ⁵³*Ibid.*, p. 77.
⁵⁴*Ibid.* ⁵⁵*Ibid.*, p. 78. ⁵⁶*Ibid.*, p. 79.
⁵⁷*Ibid.*, p. 80. ⁵⁸*Ibid.*, p. 85. ⁵⁹*Ibid.*, p. 86.
⁶⁰*Ibid.*, p. 87. ⁶¹*Ibid.*, p. 88. ⁶²*Ibid.*, pp. 89-91.
⁶³*Ibid.*, p. 92. ⁶⁴*Ibid.*, pp. 93-4. ⁶⁵*Ibid.*, p. 94.
⁶⁶*Ibid.* ⁶⁷*Ibid.*, p. 107.

⁶⁸R. Congreve, 'Moral and Social Questions Connected with our Indian Empire', *Essays: Political, Social, and Religious*, pp. 417-49.

⁶⁹Quoted in R. P. Masani, *Dadabhai Naoroji: The Grand Old Man of India* (London, 1939), pp. 229-30.

⁷⁰Dilke, *op. cit.*, p. 395. ⁷¹*Ibid.*, p. 407. ⁷²*Ibid.*, p. 389.
⁷³*Ibid.*, p. 407. ⁷⁴*Ibid.*, p. 381. ⁷⁵*Ibid.*, p. 376.
⁷⁶*Ibid.*, p. 318. ⁷⁷*Ibid.*, p. 388. ⁷⁸*Ibid.*
⁷⁹*Ibid.*, p. 380. ⁸⁰*Ibid.*, p. 207. ⁸¹*Ibid.*, p. 325.
⁸²*Ibid.*, p. 373; also p. 379. ⁸³*Ibid.*, pp. 368-9; also pp. 383-6.
⁸⁴*Ibid.*, p. 386. ⁸⁵*Ibid.*, p. 383. ⁸⁶*Ibid.*, p. 382.
⁸⁷*Ibid.*, p. 383. ⁸⁸*Ibid.*, pp. 384-5. ⁸⁹*Ibid.*, p. 388.
⁹⁰*Ibid.*, p. 389. ⁹¹*Ibid.*, pp. 257-8.

CHAPTER 4

¹J.R. Seeley, *The Expansion of England* (London, 1883), p. 11.

²E.A. Freeman, 'Imperial Federation', *Macmillan's Magazine*, April 1885, p. 444. The article is reproduced in his *Greater Greece and Greater Britain* (London, 1886), pp. 104-43.

³'Men discuss the problem of Imperial Federation as though it affected only the United Kingdom and the Colonies, forgetting that India is in population more than three-fourths of the whole Empire, and in revenue altogether before the whole of the Colonies put together.' C. W. Dilke, quoted in *Imperial Federation*, 1 April 1892, p. 78. See also Dilke's remark in his article 'An Australian View of India', *Fortnightly Review*, 1 December 1892, p. 711.

⁴*Imperial Federation*, 1 December 1893, p. 284.

⁵C.A. Bodelsen, *Studies in Mid-Victorian Imperialism* (Copenhagen, 1924), p. 168.

⁶J.A. Froude, 'England and her Colonies', *Short Studies on Great Subjects* (London, 1879), vol. ii, p. 210.

⁷E. g., H. Kilgour, *The British Empire* (London, 1869), pp. 3, 10, 13-15; E. Guthrie, *Home Rule and Federation* (Manchester, 1887), p. 6.

⁸F. Young, *Imperial Federation of Great Britain and her Colonies* (London, 1876), p. 64.

⁹See, e.g., F. P. de Labilliere, *Federal Britain* (London, 1894), pp. 102-3, 192-3; J. Colomb, M.H. Hervey and Lord Thring in *Britannic Confedera-*

tion (London, 1892), pp. 4, 130, 157-8, 164-5; H. M. Butler-Johnstone, *Imperialism, Federation and Policy* (London, 1902), p. 25.

[10] F. Young, *A Pioneer of Imperial Federation in Canada* (London, 1902), pp. 148-9.

[11] F.P. de Labilliere, *op. cit.*, pp. 103, 192-3.

[12] Of the few Anglo-Indians who took any notice of the movement before 1909, some [e.g., R. Temple, 'Imperial Federation', *Cosmopolitan Essays* (London, 1886), pp. 36-56; George Campbell, *The British Empire* (London, 1887), pp. 20ff.; J.M. Maclean's, *India's Place in an Imperial Federation* (London, 1904, pp. 7-9)] were frankly sceptical of its success, while others [e.g., C.L. Tupper, *Our Indian Protectorate* (London, 1893), pp. 380-6; D.M. Morrison, *Indian and Imperial Federation* (London, 1902), *passim*] advocated India's inclusion in an imperial *kriegsverein*.

[13] *Proceedings of the Royal Colonial Institute*, 1879-80, vol. xi, p. 169.

[14] Freeman, *Greater Greece and Greater Britain* p. 41.

[15] *Ibid.*, p. 48.

[16] *Ibid.*, 106. See also Freeman's paper 'The Physical and Political Bases of National Unity', included in *Britannic Confederation* (London, 1892), pp. 33-56; and W. R. W. Stephens, *The Life and Letters of Edward A. Freeman* (London, 1895), vol. ii, pp. 294, 356-7, 359-60, 383-4.

[17] *Bulletin*, 29 November 1890, quoted in H. L. Hall, *Australia and England* (London, 1934), pp. 141-2.

[18] Goldwin Smith, *Canada and the Canadian Question* (London, 1891), p. 258.

[19] The out-and-out federationsists generally favoured the transfer of India to the federal government. See, e.g., F.P. de Labilliere, *op. cit.*, pp. 102-3 and George R. Parkin, *Imperial Federation* (London, 1892), p. 252.

[20] J. Morley, 'The Expansion of England', *Macmillan's Magazine*, February 1884, pp. 250, 254.

[21] Goldwin Smith, *op. cit.*, p. 258.

[22] *Ibid.* For Goldwin Smith's views on the point see also his articles 'The Expansion of England', *Contemporary Review*, April 1884, pp. 524-40; 'Straining the Silken Thread', *Macmillan's Magazine*, August 1888, pp. 241-6 and 'The Empire', *Essays on Questions of the Day* (New York, 1893), pp. 127-80.

[23] G.R. Parkin, *op. cit.*, p. 243.

[24] *Asiatic Quarterly Review*, April 1892, p. 498; also October 1889, p. 290.

[25] *Ibid.*, January 1894, p. 114.   [26] *Ibid.*, p. 204.

[27] F. P. de Labilliere, *op. cit.*, p. 102.

[28] Parkin, *op. cit.*, p. 247.

[29] E.g., G. F. Bowen, 'The Federation of the British Empire', *Proceedings of the Royal Colonial Institute*, 1885-86, vol. xvii, p. 294; E. Guthrie, *Home Rule and Federation* (Manchester, 1887), p. 6; H. Mortimer-Franklyn, *The Unit of Imperial Federation* (London, 1887), pp. 210-11; W. Greswell, J. C. Fitzgerald, F. H. Turnock and C.V. Smith, in *England and her Colonies* (London, 1887), pp. 39, 60, 116, 150; T. MacFarlane, *Within the Empire* (Ottawa, 1891), pp. 68-70; S. W. Kelsey, *Imperial Federation* (London,

1903), p. 17; B.H. Thwaite, *The Electoral Government of Greater Britain* (London, 1894), p. 26; Viscount Hythe, *Problems of the Empire* (London, 1913), pp. 18, 78; *Imperial Federation*, 1 December 1892, p. 269; *British Empire Review*, November 1904, p. 103, August 1905, pp. 21-3; P. A. Silburn, *The Governance of the Empire* (London, 1910), p. 337.

30*Imperial Federation*, I July 1891, p. 163. Lord Salisbury, however, saw little hope for imperial federation, for as he wrote to Sir Henry Parkes, the premier of New South Wales, it would give the Asian parts of the Empire an overlarge voice. See C. S. Blackton, 'Australian Nationality and Nationalism: The Imperial Federationist Interlude, 1885-1901', *Historical Studies*, November 1955, p. 12.

31C.L. Tupper, 'India and Imperial Federation', *Imperial Federation*, I April 1892, p. 78. See also his book, *Our Indian Protectorate* (London, 1893), pp. 380-6.

32*Asiatic Quarterly Review*, July 1892, p. 259.

33*Ibid.*, April 1892, pp. 497-8.   34*Ibid.*, p. 496.

35'Chamberlain always seems to me Colony-mad.' Curzon to Hamilton, 24 June 1903, Hamilton Papers, India Office Library, London.

36'I often wonder what would have become of him [Chamberlain] and us, if he had ever visited India. He would have become the greatest Indian Imperialist of the time. The Colonies would have been dwarfed and forgotten and the pivot of the Empire would have been Calcutta. Not having enjoyed this good fortune we are now forgotten and the Empire is to be bound together (or, as we are told, if the prescription is not taken, destroyed) without any apparent reference to its largest most powerful unit.' Curzon to Northbrook, 12 August 1903, quoted in Ronaldshay, *The Life of Lord Curzon* (London, 1928), vol. iii, p. 24.

37*Views of the Government of India on the Question of Preferential Tariffs*, 22 *October 1903*, Cd. 1931 (1904).

38Curzon, *The Place of India in the Empire* (London, 1909), p. 46.

39The title of an address delivered by Lord Milner on 16 June 1908 before the Royal Colonial Institute. See Milner, *The Nation and the Empire* (London, 1913), pp. 289-300.

40*Ibid.*

41Jebb, *Studies in Colonial Nationalism* (London, 1905), p. 278.

42*Ibid.*, p. 278 ff.

43L.S. Amery, 'The Imperial Services', *Union and Strength* (London, 1912), pp. 54-8.

44Milner, *op. cit.*, pp. 294-9.

45This had, in fact, been one of the most favourite prescriptions of the new imperialists ever since the eighties of the 19th century.

46Morley to Minto, 28 December 1905, Morley Papers, India Office Library, London.

47Minto to Morley, 17 January 1906, *ibid.*

48The phrase is C.P. Lucas's. Objecting to Richard Jebb's proposal that India should be allowed to deal with the dominions as an equal in the 'coloured question', Lucas wrote to Jebb that 'it would tend to remove India from the field in which Canadians and Australians may exercise their joint heritage with us of ruling coloured races'. 'I want', he added, 'to gratify the Imperial—the ruling instinct of the young British peoples and it is very difficult to do this if India is made an equal with them.' Lucas to Jebb, 8 December 1913, Jebb Papers, Institute of Commonwealth Studies, University of London, London.

[49] The account which follows is based on the *Round Table Studies*, the early *Round Table* articles, the writings of Lionel Curtis, and some unpublished memoranda written by members of the group in 1912. The author is extremely grateful to Mr D. Morrah, the present editor of the *Round Table*, for permission to consult the unpublished documents in his office.

[50] The prominent members of the group were L. S. Amery, Robert Brand, Robert Cecil, Valentine Chirol, Reginald Coupland, G.L. Graik, Lionel Curtis, Geoffrey Dawson, John Dove, Patrick Duncan, Richard Feetham, Edward Grigg, Lionel Hichens, Philip Kerr, D.O. Malcolm, William Marris, James Meston, Lord Milner, F.S. Oliver, Lord Selborne, Arthur Steel-Maitland, and A. E. Zimmern.

[51] Later Lord Lothian; editor of *Round Table* 1910-16; secretary to Lloyd George 1916-21.

[52] I.C.S. 1883; lieutenant governor of United Provinces 1912-18; baron 1919.

[53] I.C.S. 1896; governor of Assam 1921-2; governor of the United Provinces 1922-7.

[54] Kerr, 'Memorandum on the Representation of India'; Marris, 'Memo. on India and the Empire'; Meston, 'Memo. on India and the Empire'. All written in June 1912 and unpublished.

[55] *Ibid.*

[56] Sir George Lillie Craik; son of Sir Henry Craik; barrister; legal adviser, Transvaal Chamber of Mines 1903-9; chief constable, Metropolitan Police 1910-14; managing director, Commonwealth Trust Ltd.

[57] Better known as Sir Dougal Malcolm; private secretary to Lord Selborne in South Africa 1905-10; president of British South Africa Company 1937-55.

[58] Craik, 'Note on the Principle of Indian Representation' (unpublished, 1912); Malcolm, 'Memorandum' (unpublished, 1912).

[59] Author; member of Milner's 'Kindergarten'; fellow of All Souls, Oxford.

[60] Curtis, 'Note on Philip Kerr's Indian Memorandum' (unpublished, 1912).

[61] Curtis, quoted in Craik, *op. cit.*, p. 4.

[62] Curtis, *op. cit.*, p. 1.

[63] In order to appreciate better the revolutionary significance of this doctrine it is necessary to recall that at almost this very time the Liberal secretary of state for India, Lord Crewe, was repeatedly affirming in Parliament that 'the maintenance and perpetual continuance of British rule in India' was the object of British policy, that he saw 'no future for India' on the lines of the self-governing colonies, and that the idea of an Indian dominion was 'a world as remote as any Atlantis or Erewhon that ever was thought of by the ingenious brain of an imaginative writer'. See 11 H. L.

Notes 149

Deb. 5 s., coll. 243-4; 12 H. L. Deb. 5s., coll. 155-6, 742-3, 745.
⁶⁴97 H. C. Deb. 5s., coll. 1295-6.
⁶⁵'Address delivered by Mr Philip Kerr at the Toronto Club, to the members of the Round Table Society—Tuesday, 30 July 1912' (unpublished), p. 12.

CHAPTER 5

¹*Proceedings of the Colonial Conference, 1887*, vol. i, C. 5091, p. 1.
²*Ibid.*, p. 371; also J. E. Kendle, *The Colonial and Imperial Conferences 1897-1911* (London, 1967), p. 8.
³*Proceedings of a Conference between the Secretary of State for the Colonies and the Premiers of the Self-Governing Colonies, 1897*, C. 8596.
⁴*Ibid.*, pp. 13-14.
⁵'Report of a Conference between the Right Hon. Joseph Chamberlain and the Premiers of the Self-Governing Colonies of the Empire at the Colonial Office in June and July 1897', Colonial Office, September 1897, Miscellaneous No. 111, Confidential, p. 130, Public Record Office (hereafter referred to as P. R. O.), London.
⁶*Ibid.*, p. 137.   ⁷*Ibid.*, p. 130.
⁸*Papers relating to a Conference between the Secretary of State for the Colonies and the Prime Ministers of Self-Governing Colonies, June-August 1902*, Cd. 1299.
⁹See copy letter from the secretary, Bengal Chamber of Commerce to the secretary, Government of India, Finance and Commerce Department, 20 June 1902: encl. Arthur Godley, under-secretary of state, India Office, to the under-secretary of state, Colonial Office, 16 July 1902, Colonial Office Records at the P.R.O., London, (hereafter referred to as C.O.) 323/475, f. 403.
¹⁰See Arthur Godley to the under-secretary of state, Colonial Office, 16 July 1902, and encl. copy letter from the under-secretary, Government of India, Finance and Commerce Department, 26 June 1902, C.O. 323/475, ff. 401, 402.
¹¹See Colonial Office minutes and copy letter from C.P. Lucas, assistant under-secretary of state, Colonial Office, to the under-secretary of state for India, 21 July 1902, C. O. 323/475, ff. 400, 404.
¹²Agreement to admit a representative of the India Office was reached after the Conference had begun its sessions, on 21 July 1902. See C.O. 323/475, f. 404. Holderness attended the Conference on 22 July, 1, 5, 8, 11 August 1902. See 'Conferenece between the Secretary of State for the Colonies and the Premiers of Self-Governing Colonies. Minutes of Proceedings and Papers Laid before the Conference', Colonial Office, October 1902, Miscellaneous No. 144, Confidential, pp. 62, 126, 145, 167, 182, P.R.O., London.
¹³'In 1902 Mr Holderness, the I. O. representative, was present at all

the meetings except the first three, and was only absent from them because the representation of the I. O. had not been settled earliers.' A. Godley to Sir F. Hopwood, 15 March 1907, C. O. 532/2, f. 9417.

[14] *Views of the Government of India on the Questions of Preferential Tariffs*, 22 October 1903, Cd. 1931 (1904).

[15] Curzon to Hamilton, 24 June 1903, Curzon Papers, India Office Library, London.

[16] Curzon to Northbrook, 12 August 1903, *ibid*.

[17] *The Times*, 17 October 1904; also 9 February, 30 October 1905, and 14 March, 1907; and *Proceedings of the Royal Colonial Institute*, 1904-5, vol. xxxvi, pp. 288-304.

[18] *British Empire Review*, August 1905, pp. 21-2.

[19] *Ibid*., November 1904, p. 103.

[20] *Correspondence relating to the Future Organization of Colonial Conferences*, Cd. 2785 (1905).

[21] *Ibid*., p. 3.

[22] E.g., C. W. Dilke, J. D. Rees and H. Cotton. See 157 H. C. Deb. 4s., coll. 940-1; 158 H. C. Deb. 4s., coll. 297, 1380; 169 H. C. Deb. 4s., coll. 721, 743.

[23] 158 H. C. Deb. 4s., col. 1380.

[24] 'We are of the opinion that India should be represented.' Campbell-Bannerman, 21 May 1906, H. C. Deb. 4s., col. 941.

[25] 158 H. C. Deb. 4s., col. 297.

[26] 169 H. C. Deb. 4s., col. 721. See also C. O. 532/2.

[27] Morley to Minto, 15 February 1907, Morley Papers, India Office Library, London.

[28] Present only on the 1st and 10th days. *Minutes of Proceedings of the Colonial Conference, 1907*, Cd. 3523, pp. 3, 295.

[29] Mackay was the regular representative of the India Office at the Conference, present on all days, except one. *Ibid*. See also A. Godley to the under-secretary of state, Colonial Office, 14 March 1907, C. O. 532/2.

[30] Present on the ninth, tenth, eleventh and twelfth days. See Cd. 3523, pp. 296, 400; and *Published Proceedingss and Precis of the Colonial Conference, 30th April to 14th May, 1907*, Cd. 3406, pp. 6, 9, 15, 18.

[31] *Papers Laid before the Colonial Conference, 1907*, Cd. 3524, pp., 453-7.

[32] Cd. 3523, pp. 297-304.

[33] *Ibid*., pp. 294, 325.

[34] 'Mr Deakin [the Australian premier] ... actually contended that India had no right to a place at the Conference table, because not self-governing. I dealt faithfully with him on the point. I laugh when I think of a man who blows the imperial trumpet louder than other people, and yet would banish India, which is the most stupendous part of the Empire—our best customer, among other triflers—into the imperial back-kitchen.' Morley to Minto, 2 May 1907, Morley Papers.

[35] When Asquith casually referred to Sir James Mackay as 'representing' India, Deakin interjected, 'He represents the British Government'. Cd. 3523, p. 294.

³⁶The Australian minister for trade and customs, Sir William Lyne, complained at the Conference: 'I do not like your absolutely ignoring the whole of the British Colonies excepting India.' *Ibid.*, p. 325.

³⁷Cd. 3523, pp. 78-89.   ³⁸*Ibid.*, p. v.

³⁹See the replies of the prime minister and the colonial secretary to questions in the Commons on 27 March and 6 April 1911, respectively. 23 H.C. Deb. 5s., coll. 899, 2420.

⁴⁰*Ibid.*, coll. 198, 397, 899, 2419-20.

⁴¹*Ibid.*, col. 397.

⁴²*Minutes of Proceedings of the Imperial Conference, 1911.* Cd. 5745, pp. 394-8.

⁴³Hardinge to Chamberlain, 29 July 1915 (telegram), Austen Chamberlain Papers, Birmingham University Library.

⁴⁴Chamberlain to Hardinge, 11, 26 August 1915 (telegrams), *ibid.*

⁴⁵*Proceedings of the Council of the Governor-General of India*, 1915-16, vol. liv, pp. 37-41.

⁴⁶*Ibid.*, pp. 42-3.   ⁴⁷*Ibid.*, p. 43.

⁴⁸*Ibid.*   ⁴⁹*Ibid.*

⁵⁰'India and the Imperial Conference', *Round Table*, December 1915, pp. 86-119.

⁵¹'Memorandum by H. E. the Viceroy upon Questions Likely to Arise in India at the End of the War', p. 25, Austen Chamberlain Papers.

⁵²*Ibid.*   ⁵³*Ibid.*, p. 26.

⁵⁴*Ibid.*, p. 25.   ⁵⁵*Ibid.*, p. 26.

⁵⁶Cited in the Government of India dispatch, Home Department, Political, No. 17, 24 November 1916, p. 10, Austen Chamberlain Papers.

⁵⁷*Ibid.*

⁵⁸Sir George Barnes, the commerce member of the government of India, told the Bengal Chamber of Commerce on 29 July 1916 that 'India's participation in the councils of the Empire had been promised definitely by the Secretary of State for India and the Prime Minister'. *The Times*, 31 July 1916. This was an obvious exaggeration.

⁵⁹Curzon, *The Place of India in the Empire* (London, 1909), p. 46.

⁶⁰Chamberlain to Hardinge, 11 August 1915 (telegram), Austen Chamberlain Papers.

⁶¹'India and the Empire', *Imperial Problems* (Empire Parliamentary Association, London, 1916), p. 21.

⁶²*Ibid.*, p. 27.   ⁶³*Ibid.*

⁶⁴Sir Charles Petrie, *The Life and Letters of the Right Hon. Sir Austen Chamberlain* (London, 1940), vol. ii, p. 73.

⁶⁵*Ibid.*, p. 74.   ⁶⁶*Ibid.*

⁶⁷D. Lloyd George, *War Memoirs* (London, 1933-6), vol. iv, pp. 1737-8. See also Petrie, *op. cit.*, vol. ii, p. 74.

⁶⁸*The Times*, 27 December 1916.

⁶⁹See Chamberlain to Walter Long, 3 April 1917, and Walter Long to Chamberlain, 4 April 1917, Austen Chamberlain Papers.

⁷⁰*Imperial War Conference, 1917. Extracts from Minutes of Proceedings and Papers Laid before the Conference*, Cd. 8566, pp. 15-16.

[71] *Ibid.*, pp. 22-3.   [72] *Ibid.*, pp. 49-50, 61.

[73] See the remark made by Austen Chamberlain at a private meeting of the Empire Parliamentary Association, held on 31 July 1918, to which Sir Satyendra Sinha delivered an address on 'Indian Constitutional Reforms'. *Indian Constitutional Reforms* (Empire Parliamentary Association, London, 1918), p. 3, Austen Chamberlain Papers.

[74] Chamberlain to Chelmsford, 15 May 1917, 'Extracts from Mr. Chamberlain's Private Letters to the Viceroy', Austen Chamberlaiu Papers.

[75] W. K. Hancock, *Survey of British Commonwealth Affairs*, vol. i, *Problems Nationality* (Oxford, 1937), p. 169.

[76] 97 H. C. Deb. 5s., coll. 1295-6.

[77] Lloyd George revealed in the Commons on 7 November 1929: 'We decided in the Imperial War Cabinet, as it was then in 1917—this country with the Prime Ministers of all the Dominions present—that there should be accorded to the people of India a considerable measure of self-government, limited, restricted, experimental, tentative, but we promised ... that gradually, if the experiment were successful, we should extend it until India ultimately enjoyed full partnership in the Empire on equal terms with our great Dominions.' 231 H. C. Deb. 5s., coll. 1314-16.

[78] Lloyd George, *op. cit.*, vol. iv, pp. 1763-4.

[79] See below, pp. 119-20.

CHAPTER 6

[1] Smith to Morley, 26 December 1906, Morley Papers, India Office Library, London.

[2] Morley to Minto, 2 August 1906, *ibid.*

[3] 161 H. L. Deb. 4s., col. 587.

[4] Morley, *Indian Speeches* (London, 1909), p. 36.

[5] Morley's oft-quoted remark: 'If it could be said that this chapter of reforms led directly or necessarily up to the establishment of a parliamentary system in India, I, for one, would have nothing to do with it ... if my existence, either officially or corporeally, were prolonged twenty times longer than either of them is likely to be a parliamentary system in India is not the goal to which I for one moment would aspire.' 198 H. L. Deb. 4s., col. 1985.

[6] Morley to Minto, 6 June 1906, Morley Papers.

[7] '... how intensely artificial and unnatural is our mighty Raj, and it sets one wondering whether it can possibly last. It surely cannot ....' Morley to Minto, 15 August 1907, *ibid.*

[8] C. H. Philips, *India* (London, 1949), p. 107.

[9] Two Indians were appointed to the council of the secretary of state and one Indian each to the executive councils of the governor-general and the governors.

[10] The number of 'additional members' was increased to a maximum of 50 in the larger and 30 in the smaller provinces. In Bombay, for example, of the total membership of 47, 5 were ex-officio members, 21 were nominated

(of which not more than 14 could be officials), and 21 were elected. All provincial legislative councils now had non-official (nominated+elected) majorities. Bengal even had a clear elected majority. The central legislative council also received an addition of Indian members, but there an official majority was retained. All the legislative councils were allowed more time to discuss the budget, to move resolutions, and to call for a division. The right of interpellation was extended and members could ask supplementary questions.

[11] *Proposals of the Government of India and Despatch of the Secretary of State*, Cd. 4426 (1908), p. 50.

[12] 'Do you know something said by Deak, the Hungarian statesman? "I can answer for today, I can pretty well for tomorrow, the day after tomorrow I leave to Providence." So do I.' Morley to Minto, 15 July 1909, Morley Papers.

[13] Minto to Morley, 17 June 1909, Morley Papers.

[14] Minto to Morley, 25 February 1909, *ibid*.

[15] 1 H. L. Deb. 5s., coll. 118-19.

[16] G. K. Gokhale, 'East and West in India', *Hindustan Review*, July 1911, p. 9.

[17] The Bishop of Southampton, 'The Unrest in India and Some of its Causes', *The East and the West*, January 1908, pp. 1-20.

[18] 'Britain's Future in India', *The Times*, 28 June 1909; *The History of The Times* (London, 1952), vol. iv, pt. ii, p. 834.

[19] Curtis, *Dyarchy* (London, 1920), p. 41.

[20] Meston, 'Memo. on India and the Empire' (unpublished), p. 2, Curtis Papers. Quoted with the kind permission of Mr D. Morrah.

[21] 37 H. L. Deb. 5s., col. 1034; C. Ilbert and J. Meston, *The New Constitution of India* (London, 1923), pp. 94-5.

[22] 19 H. C. Deb. 5s., coll. 2043-4.

[23] *Announcements by and on behalf of His Majesty the King-Emperor at the Coronation Durbar held at Delhi on December 12, 1911, with the Correspondence relating thereto*, Cd. 5979, p. 7. The dispatch was in connexion with the proposed transfer of the capital of India from Calcutta to Delhi.

[24] *Speeches on Indian Questions* (Madras, 1918), pp. 247-59.

[25] 11 H. L. Deb. 5s., coll. 243-4.

[26] 12 H. L. Deb. 5s., coll. 155-6.

[27] *Ibid*., coll. 742-3.   [28] *Ibid*., col. 745.

[29] 12 H. L. Deb. 5s., coll. 748-51.

[30] William Archer, *India and the Future* (London, 1917), p. 295.

[31] *Indian Review*, January 1913, p. 54.

[32] 'India and the Empire', *Round Table*, September 1912, pp. 623-5; J.R.M. Butler, *Lord Lothian* (London, 1960), p. 175.

[33] *Round Table*, December 1912, p. 52.

[34] See, for example, the evidence of Sir Claude H. Hill, ex-member of the executive council of the governor of Bombay and of the governor-general of India, before the Joint Select Committee in 1919; *Report of the Joint Select Committee on the Government of India Bill*, H. C. 203, 1919, vol. i, p. 31.

[35] V. Srinivasa Sastri, *Life of Gopal Krishna Gokhale* (Madras, 1937), pp. 112-13.

[36] Willingdon to Lloyd George, 22 January 1916, Lloyd George, *War Memoirs* (London, 1933-6), vol. iv, p. 1739.

[37] The phrase quoted is Sir S. P. Sinha's. See *Speeches and Writings of Lord Sinha* (Madras, 1919), p. 86.

[38] *Report of the Thirtieth Indian National Congress, 1915*, pp. 21-30.

[39] 69 H. L. Deb. 5s., coll. 266-7; C. H. Setalvad, *Recollections and Reflections* (Bombay, 1946), p. 248.

[40] 'Memorandum by H.E. the Viceroy upon Questions Likely to Arise in India at the End of the War', Austen Chamberlain Papers, Birmingham University Library. The main recommendations of Hardinge were: (*i*) commissions for Indians in the army; (*ii*) modification of the Arms Act; (*iii*) abolition of the Indian excise duty on cotton goods; (*iv*) modification of the regulations of the central and provincial legislative councils (elected majority in the provinces, increase of elected members at the centre, wider electorates); (*v*) relaxation of control exercised by the centre over the provinces, and by the secretary of state over the government of India; (*vi*) India's representation at the Imperial Conference; (*vii*) abolition of indentured labour; (*viii*) state-aid for Indian industries; (*ix*) appointment of Indians to the privy council; and (*x*) increased employment of Indians in the public services.

[41] *Times of India*, 11 October 1915.

[42] *Proceedings of the Council of the Governor-General of India, 1915-16*, vol. liv, p. 559.

[43] The prominent members of the group were L. S. Amery, Robert Brand, Robert Cecil, Valentine Chirol, Reginald Coupland, G. L. Craik, Lionel Curtis, Geoffrey Dawson, John Dove, Patrick Duncan, Richard Feetham, Edward Grigg, Lionel Hichens, Philip Kerr, D. O. Malcolm, William Marris, James Meston, Lord Milner, F. S. Oliver, Lord Selborne, Arthur Steel-Maitland, and A. E. Zimmern.

The account of the activities of the Round Table group which follows is based on Curtis, *Dyarchy*, pp. xx ff. and the Curtis Papers. For permission to make use of the latter the author is indebted to Mr D. Morrah. [See also D.C. Ellinwood, 'The Round Table Movement and India, 1909-1920', *Journal of Commonwealth Political Studies*, November 1971, pp. 183-209, and J. Kendle, *The Round Table and Imperial Union* (Toronto, 1975).]

[44] Curtis, *op. cit.*, p. xxii.

[45] Originally issued under the title, *Suggestions for Constitutional Progress in Indian Polity*, it later beame famous as 'the Duke Memorandum'.

[46] See the remark made by Crewe in the Lords on 12 December 1919. 37 H. L. Deb. 5s., col. 986.

[47] *Proceedings of the Indian Legislative Council*, 1917-18, vol. lvi, p. 17.

[48] *Ibid.*, pp. 17-18.

[49] Government of India, Home Department, Political, No. 17, 24 November 1917, Austen Chamberlain Papers.

[50] *Ibid.*, pp. 19-24.

⁵¹See Chelmsford to Chamberlain, 30 May 1917 (telegram), Austen Chamberlain Papers. Also, 69 H. L. Deb. 5s., coll. 267-8.
⁵²Government of India, Home Department, Political, No. 17, 24 November 1917, p. 20, Austen Chamberlain Papers.
⁵³*Ibid.*, p. 16.
⁵⁴*Proceedings of the Indian Legislative Council*, 1916-17, vol. lv, pp. 45-6, 51.
⁵⁵*Times of India*, 30 December 1916; 1-2 January 1917. The other main demands of the Congress and the League were: (*i*) provincial autonomy; (*ii*) four-fifths of the central and provincial legislative councils to be elected; (*iii*) not less than half the members of the central and provincial governments to be elected by their respective legislative councils; (*iv*) the executives to be bound to act in accordance with the resolutions passed by their legislative councils unless they were vetoed by the governor-general or governors, in that event, if the resolution were passed again after an interval of not less than one year, it should in any case be put into effect; (*v*) the relations of the secretary of state with the government of India to be similar to those of the colonial secretary with the dominion governments, and India to have an equal status with the dominions in any body concerned with imperial affairs.
⁵⁶K.M. Panikkar, *His Highness the Maharaja of Bikaner: A Biography* (London, 1937), p. 174.
⁵⁷*Times of India*, 15 May 1917.
⁵⁸*Ibid.*, 21 June 1917. Also 2 August 1917.
⁵⁹*Indian Review*, August 1917, p. 542.
⁶⁰*Nineteenth Century and After*, August 1916, pp. 265-83; *Indian Review*, July 1917, pp. 449-54.
⁶¹'Report on Government of India Despatch, Home Department, No. 17, Political, dated November 24, 1916', 16 March 1917, Austen Chamberlain papers.
⁶²*Ibid.*, pp. 1-2.   ⁶³*Ibid.*, p. 7.
⁶⁴*Ibid.*   ⁶⁵*Ibid.*, p. 8.
⁶⁶'After all, we want to train Indians in self-government. A mere increase in the number of their representatives does not really advance this object, unless we can at the same time fix these men with some definite powers and with real respnosibility for their actions.' Chamberlain to Chelmsford, 2 May 1917, 'Extracts from Mr Chamberlain's Private Letters to the Viceroy', Austen Chamberlain Papers. Again, on 15 May 1917, Chamberlain wrote to Chelmsford: 'My difficulty in regard to this scheme is, first, that it makes no real progress towards self-government; and, secondly, that it will perpetuate and aggravate a vicious system which makes it the main function of the Legislative Councils to oppose and criticise the Government while remaining completely free from responsibility for the results of their action.... The vital difficulty of this scheme, as it seems to me, is that, while increasing the number of representatives, it does nothing to secure any increase in their sense of responsibility; it gives them no real training in affairs and will merely multiply the number of irresponsible critics who, dissatisfied with their own impotence and deprived of all sense of responsibility for their actions, may become a grave embarrassment to Government. I can see no use in multiplying elected representatives until we are prepared to entrust

them with some degree of responsibility in financial or administrative matters.' *Ibid.*

[67]'I am coming round to your view that a statement of our object is necessary.' Chamberlain to Chelmsford, 2 May 1917, Austen Chamberlain Papers.

[68] Chamberlain to Chelmsford, 15 May 1917, *ibid.*

[69] Chelmsford to Chamberlain, 2 May 1917, *ibid.*

[70] *The Times*, 2 May 1917.

[71] See the remark of Bikaner to this effect, reproduced in *Speeches and Writings of Lord Sinha*, Appendix, pp. xix-xx. Also K. M. Panikkar, *op. cit.*, pp. 185-9; 'Memorandum by H. H, the Maharaja of Bikaner', dated 17 April 1917, Austen Chamberlain Papers; 'Note on Constitutional Reforms in India', May 1917, by Meston, *ibid.*; Chamberlain to Chelmsford, 8 May 1917 (reporting a talk with Sinha), 'Extracts from Mr Chamberlain's Private Letters to the Viceroy', *ibid.*

[72] On this point see Lloyd George, *op. cit.*, vol. iv, pp. 1763-4 and 231 H. C. Deb. 5s., coll. 1314-16.

[73] See above, p. 83.

[74] See Chamberlain to Chelmsford, 27 November 1916, and Chelmsford to Chamberlain, 1 December 1916 (telegrams), Austen Chamberlain Papers.

[75] Chelmsford to Chamberlain, 18 May 1917 (telegram), *ibid.*

[76] Telegram from the Viceroy to the Secretary of State, Home Department, 18 May 1917, 'Indian Political Reforms, Collection of Telegrams (unparaphrased) between Viceroy and Secretary of States', pp. 1-3, Austen Chamberlain Papers.

[77]'Memorandum by the Secretary of State for India on Indian Reforms', *ibid.*

[78] Austen Chamberlain, *Down the Years* (London, 1935), p. 132.

[79] Lord Ronaldshay, *The Life of Lord Curzon* (London, 1928), vol. iii, p. 164. Ronaldshay did not disclose the name of Balfour, but simply referred to him as 'one prominent member of the Cabinet'. It is significant that Curzon considered Balfour's note to be 'very stubborn and rather reactionary'. See Curzon to Chamberlain, 25 August 1917, Austen Chamberlain Papers.

[80] A royal commission which inquired into the mismanagement of the campaign in Mesopotamia revealed a very disquieting state of affairs, particularly where the medical services were concerned, and accused the government of India of administrative inefficiency. There was never any suggestion that blame attached to Austen Chamberlain, but he was secretary of state for India, and as it was his department which was involved he felt it to be his duty to resign.

[81] 95 H. C. Deb., 5s., coll. 2202-10. [82] *Times of India*, 30 July 1917.

[83] 26 H. L. Deb. 5s., col. 768; 31 H. L. Deb. 5s., col. 597.

[84]'Indian Reforms', encl. Montagu to Chamberlain, 7 August 1917, Austen Chamberlain Papers.

[85] See Montagu to Chamberlain, 7 August 1917, *ibid.* On 15 August 1917, Montagu wrote to Chamberlain: 'The number of times that I have sat trembling for a Cabinet summons, the number of times that I have hoped

Notes

to see the Prime Minister, the number of messages that I have got from the Viceroy,—all this would make a story which would bring tears to your eyes. . . .' *Ibid.*

[86] F. Owen, *Tempestuous Journey: Lloyd George, His Life and Times* (London, 1955), p. 416.

[87] See Montagu to Chamberlain, 7 August 1917, and encl., *op. cit.*, p. 2, Austen Chamberlain Papers.

[88] 'Indian Reforms', *op. cit.*, p. 3, *ibid.*; and Ronaldshay, *op. cit.*, vol. iii, p. 167.

[89] Montagu to Chamberlain, 7 August 1917, Austen Chamberlain Papers.

[90] Ronaldshay, *op. cit.*, vol. iii, p. 168.

[91] *Ibid.*, p. 167. It is not possible, in the present stage of our knowledge, to account precisely for the choice of the phrase 'responsible government' in preference to 'self-government' by Curzon and the cabinet. The following comments by Montagu on the point are interesting, but not very enlightening. 'For some reason which I am absolutely unable to understand people prefer "responsible Government" to "Self-government". I do not know the difference. If there is a difference, "Self-government" might mean that India was to be placed under a Hindu or Parsee dictator, but "responsible Government", I should have thought, meant that that Hindu or Parsee dictator would have been responsible to some form of Parliamentary institution. So I think they [the cabinet] have given more than your formula would have necessitated.' Montagu to Chamberlain, 15 August 1917, Austen Chamberlain Papers. 'It was a strange discussion. I had hoped that the word "self-government" would be used, because it appeared in every one of your communications and because I thought it was a pity to boggle at a word so current in Indian discussion. The Cabinet in its wisdom preferred the words 'responsible Government' to "Self-Goverment". It requires a better educated man than myself to know the difference, but if it lies anywhere, "responsible Government", I should have thought, pledges more than "self-Government".' Montagu to Chelmsford, 21 August 1917, Sir David Waley, 'Life of the Hon. Edwin Samuel Montagu' (unpublished), p. 174. quoted with the kind permission of the author. [For further discussion on this point in the light of fresh evidence become available since this article was written in 1963, see Richard Danzig, 'The Announcement to August 20th, 1917', *Journal of Asian Studies*, November 1968, pp. 19-37, and Peter Robb, 'The British Cabinet and Indian Reform, 1917-19', *Journal of Imperial and Commonwealth History*, May 1976, pp. 318-34.]

[92] 97 H. C. Deb. 5s., coll. 1995-6.

[93] *Report on Indian Constitutional Reforms*, 1918, Cd. 9109, p. 5.

[94] The phrase is Lord Milner's. See his *The Nation and the Empire* (London, 1913), p. 289.

[95] A. E. Zimmern, *The Third British Empire* (London, 1926).

CHAPTER 7

[1] D. G. Tendulkar, *Mahatma* (Bombay, 1951), vol. i, p. 280.

[2] K. Dwarkadas, *Gandhiji through my Diary Leaves* (Bombay, 1950), pp. 10-11.
[3] Tendulkar, *op. cit.*, vol. i, p. 278.
[4] Montagu, *An Indian Diary*, (London, 1930), p. 58.
[5] Tendulkar, *op. cit.*, vol. i, p. 278.
[6] *Ibid.*, p. 282.
[7] *Young India*, 28 July 1920.
[8] C.F. Andrews, *Mahatma Gandhi's Ideas* (London, 1929), p. 249.
[9] If is generally believed that the viceroy, Lord Reading, privately offered in December 1921 to grant full responsible government to the provinces immediately and to convene a conference of Indian leaders to discuss other outstanding issues. Gandhi insisted that the Khilafat leaders, Mohamed Ali and Shaukat Ali, who were then in jail, should be invited to the proposed conference. The viceroy refused to do so and withdrew the offer, Lord Llyod, the then governor of Bombay, commented later: 'Gandhi's was the most colossal experiment in world history, and it came within an inch of succeeding.' quoted by C.F. Andrews, 'Heart Beats in India', *Asia*, March 1930, p. 198.
[10] *Young India*, 13 July 1921.
[11] *Ibid.*, 6 April 1921; 19 January, 23 February 1922.
[12] *Ibid.*, 6 October 1920.
[13] *Ibid.*, 29 June 1921.
[14] S.L. Karandikar, *Lokmanya Bal Gangadhar Tilak* (Poona, 1957), p. 635.
[15] Andrews, *How India Can Be Free* (Madras, 1921); *Indian Independence: The Immediate Need* (Madras, 1921); *The Indian Problem* (Madras, 1921); *The Claim for Independence Within or Without the British Empire* (Madras, 1921). See also his introduction to S. E. Stokes, *The Failure of European Civilization as a World Culture* (Madras, 1921) and B. Chaturvedi and M. Sykes, *Charles Freer Andrews* (London, 1949), pp. 155-6.
[16] '... it seemed to me not only to make an unanswerable case for independence but also to mirror the inmost recesses of our hearts. The deep urge that moved us and our half-formed desires seemed to take a clear shape in his simple and earnest language.... It was wonderful that C. F. Andrews, a foreigner and one belonging to the dominant race in India, should echo the cry of our inmost being.' J. Nehru, *An Autobiography* (London, 1942), p. 66.
[17] Andrews, Introduction to *Speeches and Writings of M. K. Gandhi* (Madras, 1922), pp. xv-vi.
[18] *Young India*, 5 January 1922.
[19] *Ibid*.
[20] *Report of the Thirty-ninth Indian National Congress, 1924*, p. 26.
[21] *Ibid*.
[22] *Times of India*, 30 December 1926.
[23] Tendulkar, *op. cit.*, vol. ii, p. 402.
[24] *Young India*, 12 January 1928.
[25] *Indian Quarterly Register*, 1929, vol. ii, p. 300.
[26] *Ibid.*, p. 302.

27 Gandhi, *Speeches and Writings* (Madras, 1933), pp. 734, 739.
28 H. Nicolson, *King George the Fifth* (London, 1952), p. 508.
29 Gandhi told Irwin: 'I want to see India established in her own self-respect and in the respect of the world. I, therefore, want to see India able to discuss with Great Britain on terms of equality, and Great Britain willing to discuss with India on such terms. I know perfectly well that we want British help in many things for a long time yet—defence, administration and so on—and I am prepared to have safeguards, or as I prefer to call them, adjustments, provided these are really in the interests of India.... If we can reach agreement on those lines, I shall be satisfied that I have got *Purna Swaraj* or complete independence, and India will have got it is what to me is the highest form in which it can be attained, namely, in association with Great Britain. But if Great Britain will not help me in this way, and if this achievement in partnership cannot be brought about, then I must pursue my end of *Purna Swaraj* or complete independence in isolation from Great Britain, and this I definitely regard as the second best.' *Ibid.*
30 Indian Round Table Conference, Second Session: *Proceedings of the Federal Structure Committee and Minorities Committee*, 1932, p. 17.
31 *Ibid.*
32 Indian Round Table Conference, Second Session: *Proceedings*. Cmd. 3997 (1932), p. 393.
33 'It [independence] need not be different from dominion status.... If dominion status could be so defined as to cover a case like India and India could come to a honourable agreement with England, I would not quarrel about words.' Tendulkar, *op. cit.*, vol. v, pp. 137-8. See also H. S. L. Polak and others, *Mahatma Gandhi* (London, 1949), p. 75.
34 'There was a time when I was enamoured of dominion status, but I found that dominion status is a status common to members of the same family—Australia, Canada, South Africa, New Zealand, etc. These are daughter states in a sense that India is not.' Gandhi quoted in C. Rajagopalachari and J.C. Kumarappa (eds.), *The Nation's Voice* (Ahmedabad, 1947), p. 126.
35 V.P. Menon, *The Transfer of Power in India* (London, 1957), p. 74.
36 L.S. Amery on Gandhi, quoted in S. Radhakrishnan (ed.), *Mahatma Gandhi* (London, 1949), p. 524.
37 J. Nehru, *op. cit.*, p. 418.
38 E.g., Sir Stanley Reed, *The India I Knew* (London, 1952), p. 57.
39 Pyarelal, *Mahatma Gandhi—The Last Phase* (Ahmedabad, 1957-8), vol. ii, p. 160.
40 Tendulkar, *op. cit.*, vol. viii, p. 168.
41 Pyarelal, *op. cit.*, vol. ii, p. 167.
42 Radhakrishnan (ed.), *op. cit.*, p. 524.
43 Cmd. 3997, p. 394.
44 *Proceedings of the Federal Structure Committee and Minorities Committee*, p. 17.
45 Pyarelal, *op. cit.*, vol. i, p. 172; vol. ii, p. 98.
46 Tendulkar, *op. cit.*, vol. viii, p. 75.
47 Pyarelal, *op. cit.*, vol. ii, p. 304.

CHAPTER 8

[48] Tendulkar, *op. cit.*, vol. viii, pp. 62-3.
[49] For a brilliant appraisal of Gandhi and his methods by Smuts, see Radhakrishnan (ed.), *op. cit.*, pp. 280-5.

[1] *Constituent Assembly Debates*, vol. ii, p. 324.
[2] See S. R. Mehrotra, *India and the Commonwealth 1885-1929* (London, 1965), p. 138.
[3] *Ibid.*
[4] *Ibid.*, p. 142.
[5] J. Nehru, *An Autobiography* (Bombay, 1962), p. 612.
[6] J. Nehru, *Glimpses of World History* (Bombay, 1962), pp. 717-18.
[7] J. Nehru, *India and the World* (London, 1936), pp. 204-5.
[8] S. R. Mehrotra, *India and the Commonwealth 1885-1929*, p. 139.
[9] *Ibid.*, pp. 145-6.
[10] J. Nehru, *An Autobiography*, pp. 418-19.
[11] J. Nehru, *The Discovery of India* (Bombay, 1961), p. 495.
[12] *Jawaharlal Nehru's Speeches* (Delhi, 1954-68), vol. i, p. 3.
[13] *Ibid.*, pp. 13-15.
[14] *Ibid.*, pp. 21-2.
[15] N. Mansergh (ed.), *Documents and Speeches on British Commonwealth Affairs 1931-1952* (London, 1953), vol. ii, p. 660.
[16] *Jawaharlal Nehru's Speeches*, vol. i, pp. 13-15, 20-1, 38-9.
[17] *Ibid.*, pp. 13, 19.
[18] N. Mansergh, *The Commonwealth Experience* (London, 1969), p. 329.
[19] See A. Campbell-Johnson, *Mission with Mountbatten* (London, 1951), pp. 72, 81, 87, 88, 109, 129, 214, 219, 242, 255, 257, 269, 290-1, 310-11, 329; N. Mansergh, The *Commonwealth Experience*, pp. 329-30; V. P. Menon, *The Transfer of Power in India* (Bombay, 1968), p. 448.
[20] N. Mansergh, *The Commonwealth Experience*, p. 337.
[21] *Jawaharlal Nehru's Speeches*, vol. i, pp. 268-9.
[22] *Ibid.*, pp. 38-9.
[23] N.V. Rajkumar (ed.), *The Background of India's Foreign Policy*, (New Delhi, 1952), p. 96.
[24] For the evolution of the formula, see H. Duncan Hall, *Commonwealth* (London, 1971), pp. 831-62; N. Mansergh, *The Commonwealth Experience*, pp. 333-6; P. Gordon Walker, *The Commonwealth* (London, 1965), pp. 137-9, 182-5; M. Brecher, *India and World Politics* (London, 1968), pp. 18-27; and Durga Das (ed.), *Sardar Patel's Correspondence 1945-50* (Ahmedabad, 1971-4), vol. 8, pp. 1-25.
[25] The full text is available in N. Mansergh (ed.), *Documents and Speeches on British Commonwealth Affairs*, vol. ii, pp. 846-7.
[26] *Constituent Assembly Debates*, vol. viii, p. 72.
[27] N. V. Rajkumar (ed.), *The Background of India's Foreign Policy*, p. 98.
[28] N. Mansergh, *Survey of British Commonwealth Affairs: Problems of Wartime Co-operation and Post-War Change 1939-1952* (London, 1958), p. 252; also N. Mansergh, *The Commonwealth Experience*, p. 336.

[29]See above, pp. 73-4.
[30]M. Brecher, *Nehru: A Political Biography* (London, 1959), p. 415.
[31]S.R. Mehrotra, *India and the Commonwealth 1885-1929*, pp. 122-6.
[32]*Ibid.*, pp. 142-3.
[33]*Ibid.*, pp. 144-5. See also Chapter 7, above.
[34]Quoted in A. Campbell-Johnson, *Mission with Mountbatten*, p. 353.
[35]*Jawaharlal Nehru's Speeches*, vol. i, p. 284.
[36]N. Mansergh (ed.), *Documents and Speeches on British Commonwealth Affairs*, vol. ii, p. 616.
[37]*Jawaharlal Nehru's Speeches*, vol. i, pp. 268, 282, vol. iii, pp. 314, 316; also R.K. Karanjia, *The Mind of Mr Nehru* (London, 1960), pp. 91-2. On the role of India in transforming the Commonwealth see M.S. Rajan, *The Post-War Transformation of the Commonwealth* (Bombay, 1963), passim, and J.D.B. Miller, *Survey of Commonwealth Affairs: Problems of Expansion and Attrition 1953-1969* (London, 1974), pp. 11-13.
[38]On 16 May 1949 Nehru said: 'In the world today where there are so many disruptive forces at work, where we are often on the verge of war, I think it is not a safe thing to encourage the breaking up of any association that one has. Break up the evil part of it, break up anything that may come in the way of your growth, because nobody dare agree to anything that comes in the way of a nation's growth. Otherwise. ... It is better to keep going a co-operative association. ... Some people have thought that by joining or continuing to remain in the Commonwealth of Nations we are drifting away from our neighbours in Asia, or that it has become more difficult for us to co-operate with other countries, great countries in the world. But I think it is easier for us to develop closer relations with other countries while we are in the Commonwealth than it might have been otherwise. This is rather a peculiar thing to say. Nevertheless, I say it, and I have given a great deal of thought to this matter.' *Jawaharlal Nehru's Speeches*, vol. i, pp. 281, 285.
[39]A. Campbell-Johnson and H. V. Hodson suggest that the fear of some of the recalcitrant Indian princely states declaring their independence and seeking separate Commonwealth membership might have been a makeweight in determining Nehru's policy of keeping India in the Commonwealth in 1947-8. See A. Campbell-Johnson, *Mission with Mountbatten*, pp. 88, 135, 329; and H.V. Hodson, *The Great Divide* (London, 1969), p. 379.
[40]B. N. Rau, *India's Constitution in the Making* (Bombay, 1960), p. 344.
[41]*Jawaharlal Nehru's Speeches*, vol. i, p. 285.
[42]*Ibid.*, p. 281.
[43]Speaking in the Lok Sabha on 3 February 1950, Nehru remarked: 'Apart from the general reason, namely, that there is absolutely no object in our breaking an association which might help and certainly cannot hinder and which helps in the larger context of world affairs, there is one major reason for our remaining in the Commonwealth and that is that a large number of Indians live abroad in what are called British colonies or dependencies. ... By our remaining in the Commonwealth, these Indians are in a better position than they would be otherwise. In the latter case, they would

have to make a sudden choice and break with India or with the country where they reside. Had we left the Commonwealth it would have put millions of our people in a very difficult position, quite unnecessarily.' *Jawaharlal Nehru's Speeches*, vol. ii, p. 130.

[44] N. Mansergh, *The Commonwealth Experience*, p. 393. Selwyn Lloyd, the British foreign secretary, on the other hand, remarked in 1956 that Nehru was 'one of the ablest expounders of what the Commonwealth really means at the present time'. See *Hindu*, 6 July 1956, quoted in M. S. Rajan, *India in World Affairs 1954-56* (Bombay, 1964), p. 350.

[45] *Jawaharlal Nehru's Speeches*, vol. i, p. 287.

[46] N. Mansergh, *The Commonwealth Experience*, p. 394. Speaking in the Indian Constituent Assembly on 17 May 1949, Nehru claimed that his decision to keep India in the Commonwealth would 'have met with the approval of Gandhiji'. See *Jawaharlal Nehru's Speeches*, vol. i, p. 292.

[47] *Jawaharlal Nehru's Speeches*, vol. i, p. 279.

[48] See P. Gordon Walker, *The Commonwealth*, pp. 175-6.

[49] *Jawaharlal Nehru's Speeches*, vol. ii, p. 129.

[50] *Hindu*, 6 July 1956, quoted in M.S. Rajan, *India in World Affairs 1954-56*, pp. 342-3.

[51] *Jawaharlal Nehru's Speeches*, vol. ii, p. 129. Speaking in the Lok Sabha on 5 December 1956, Nehru observed: 'India can be influenced by other countries, but it should be remembered that India also can influence other countries, and has done so to a remarkable extent in the past few years.' *Ibid.*, vol. iii, p. 316.

[52] See J.D.B. Miller, *The Commonwealth in the World* (London, 1958), pp. 155-8.

INDEX

Abrahams, Sir Lionel, 86
Acton, Lord, 14
Adderley, Sir Charles, 21
Adelaide, 4, 5
Africa, 11, 111, 127
Alexander, Horace, 107
All-India Muslim League, 81, 89, 94, 102, 117
All-Parties Conference Report, 103
America. *See* United States of America
Amery, L.S., 56
Amritsar, 98
Amritsar massacre, 98, 106
Andrews, C.F., 99, 100-1, 105
Anglo-Irish Treaty 1921, 16, 111
Arabia, 70
Archer, William, 81
Asia, 11, 35, 38, 111, 123, 127
Asian Relations Conference, 123
Asiatic Quarterly Review, 52, 54
Asquith, H.H., 66, 67, 69
Attlee, C.R., 115, 116
Australasia, 23
Australia, 2, 4, 5, 7, 9, 11, 36, 54, 66, 72, 112

Balfour, Lord, 93
Balfour Committee Report, 102
Barker, E., 27
Barton, Sir Edmund, 17
Belgaum, 102

Bengal Chamber of Commerce, 63
Besant, Annie, 83, 92, 93, 97-8
Bikaner, Maharaja of, 73, 89, 91
Birkenhead, Lord, 103
Board of Control, 23
Board of Trade and Plantations, 22
Bodelsen, C.A., 33
Boers, 19, 30, 102, 111
Boer War. *See* South African War
Bombay, 84, 92, 94
Borden, Sir Robert, 15, 16, 72, 73
Bose, Subhas Chandra, 104
Botha, General, 72
Bright, John, 24, 37, 38, 40-1, 48
British Commonwealth; British Commonwealth of Nations. *See* Commonwealth
British Empire, 4, 5, 6, 7, 8, 9, 10, 12, 13, 14, 15, 18, 19, 24, 25, 26, 27, 28, 29, 31, 36, 37, 39, 48, 50, 51, 52, 54, 56, 58, 60, 62, 63, 64, 67, 70, 71, 72, 74, 75, 82, 85, 88, 90, 91, 93, 95, 96, 97, 99, 100, 101, 105, 110, 111, 112, 113
British Empire League, 6, 65
Bryce, James, 2
Bulletin, 52
Burke, Edmund, 3, 26, 31, 40
Burma, 120
Burnet, Gilbert, 1

Cabinet Mission, 116
Calcutta, 47, 63, 76

Campbell-Bannerman, Sir Henry, 11, 66
Canada, 7, 9, 19, 28, 34, 52, 54, 66, 72, 112
Cape Colony, 5, 37
Ceylon, 37
Chamberlain, Austen, 68, 71, 72, 73, 91, 92-3, 94, 95
Chamberlain, Joseph, 7, 11, 54, 55, 62-3, 64, 65
Charles I, 2
Charter Act 1833, 27
Chartist movement, 28
Chelmsford, Lord, 70, 73, 85, 87, 89, 91, 98
Childs, W.M., 9
China, 44, 110
Churchill, Winston, 30, 115
Cobden, Richard, 34, 36, 37-9, 48
Colonial Conference, 6, 10; 1887: 62; 1897: 54, 62-3; 1902: 54, 63-4, 65; 1907: 8, 10, 55, 66-7
Colonial Development and Welfare Act 1940, 27
Colonial Office, 22, 54, 65
Colonies, 5, 6, 7, 8, 18, 19, 24, 33, 34, 35, 43, 49-50, 53, 54, 56, 57, 62, 63, 65, 66, 67, 76. *See also* Dominions
Commonwealth, 1, 4, 5, 6, 11, 12, 13, 15, 16, 17, 31, 59, 60, 61, 74, 86, 100, 105, 106, 107, 108, 109, 110, 111, 113, 115, 116, 117, 118, 119, 121, 122, 123, 124, 126
Commonwealth of nations, 4, 5, 14, 96, 101, 110, 118, 119
Commonwealth of Nations, The, 15
Commonwealth or Empire, 12
Commonwealth Prime Ministers' Conference, 118, 120, 125
Complete independence, 100, 103, 105, 110, 111, 119, 121
Congress. *See* Indian National Congress
Congress Democratic Party, 100
Congress-League scheme of reforms, 94
Congreve, Richard, 24, 37, 41-5, 48

Conservatives (British), 57, 122
Corn Laws, 24, 39
Cotton, Sir Henry, 66
Coupland, Reginald, 86
Courtney, Lord, 81
Craik, G.L., 58
Crewe, Lord, 81, 83
Cripps proposals, 123
Cromwell, Oliver, 3
Cross, Lord, 62
Curtis, Lionel, 10, 13, 15, 58-60, 79, 86
Curzon, Lord, 8, 54, 63, 64, 71, 80, 95

Danubian principalities, 42
Delhi, 113, 123
Denmark, 42
Dilke, C.W., 19, 36, 37, 45-8, 49
Disraeli, Benjamin, 11, 34
Dominions, 10, 13, 18, 22, 25, 27, 28, 30, 33, 60, 67, 68, 69, 70, 71, 72, 73, 74, 81-2, 84, 86, 88, 95, 100, 101, 108, 111, 112, 113, 118
Dominion status, 100, 102, 103, 104, 105, 107, 110, 111, 113, 117, 121
Downing Street, 10, 72
Dryden, John, 3
Dudley, Edmund, 1
Dufferin, Lord, 28-9
Duke memorandum, 87, 88
Duke, Sir William, 86, 87, 90
Durban, 7
Durham, Lord, 28
Dyarchy, 60, 88
Dyer, General, 98

East India Company, 18, 20, 22-3, 26, 27, 28, 35, 36, 38
Edinburgh Review, 7
Egypt, 13, 100
Eire, 111, 117
Elizabeth I, Queen, 18
Elizabeth II, Queen, 108
Empire. *See* British Empire

Index

Empire Parliamentary Association, 71
Enabling Act, 24
Enock, C.R., 13
Europe, 13, 51
Evangelicalism, 26
Exeter Hall, 37
Extremists, 80, 89, 98, 122
Ewart, J. S., 10

Fascism, 115
Fisher, Andrew, 11
France, 42
Fraser, Lovat, 78
Freeman, E. A., 3, 49, 51-2
Free trade, 24, 35, 53
French Canadians, 19, 30
Froude, J.A., 3, 9

Gandhi, Mohandas Karamchand, 97-109, 120, 125
Gauhati, 102
George V, King, 104
German Empire, 13, 14
Germany, 15, 110
Ghose, Aurobindo, 100
Gibraltar, 44
Gokhale, G.K., 30, 76, 77-8, 83, 107
Goldsmith, Oliver, 2, 3
Grenville, Lord, 27
Grey, Albert, 56-7

Hamilton, Lord George, 54, 63
Hancock, W.K., 16, 74
Hardinge, Lord, 68-9, 70, 85
Hardyng, John, 1
Harrington, Sir John, 3
Hartington, Lord, 45
Hertzog, General, 102-3
Hervey, M.H., 9
Hind Swaraj, 97
Hobbes, Thomas, 3
Holderness, T.W., 64, 66

Home rule agitation in India, 92, 97-8, 100
Home Rule agitation in Ireland, 28
Hughes, William, 72
Hunter Commission, 98
Hyderabad, 123

Imperial Conference, 10, 60, 68, 69, 70, 71, 72, 111, 119; 1911: 67; 1921: 16; 1926: 102
Imperial Federation League, 3, 49, 53
Imperial War Cabinet, 73-4
Imperial War Conference 1917, 15, 16, 31, 73, 74, 91-2
India Council, 23
Indian Civil Service, 56-7, 79
Indian Constituent Assembly, 110, 116, 117, 118, 119, 124
Indian Councils Act 1861, 28
Indian Councils Act 1892, 28, 75, 88
Indian Councils Act 1909. *See* Morley-Minto reforms
Indian National Congress, 28, 66, 76, 83, 84, 85, 89, 94, 98, 102, 103, 104, 105, 111, 113, 118, 119, 120, 121
India Office, 64, 90
Ireland, 14, 45, 111, 112, 121, 122
Irish Free State. *See* Eire
Irwin, Lord, 104
Islington, Lord, 71-2
Italy, 110

Jaipur, 118
Jebb, Richard, 7, 13, 46, 56
Jinnah, M.A., 98
Johannesburg, 7
Jung, Salar, 46

Kashmir, 108, 117, 123, 125
Kentucky, 2

Kerr, Philip, 13, 57, 58, 59, 61, 81, 86
Kisch, C.H., 86
Khilafat, 99, 100
Kipling, Rudyard, 7

Labilliere, F. P. de, 50, 53
Labour government, 115, 122
Labour party, 122
Lahore, 104, 111, 113
Lancashire, 39
Laurier, Sir Wilfrid, 10
Lewis, George Cornewall, 21, 35
Liberals (British), 57, 66
Little, J.S., 13
Lloyd George, David, 2, 72, 73, 74, 93, 94
Locke, John, 2, 3
London, 22, 39, 45, 71, 73, 87, 103, 113, 118, 119, 120, 121, 125
Long, Walter, 73
Lucas, C.P., 22, 23, 28
Lyall, Sir Alfred, 81
Lyttleton, Alfred, 65

Macaulay, T.B., 24
Mackay, Sir James, 63, 66
Malcolm, D.O., 58
Malmesbury, Lord, 34
Manchester, 37, 41
Manchester school, 25, 34
Mansergh, Nicholas, 5, 117, 119, 124
Marris, William, 57, 58, 59, 79
Massachusetts, 2
Massey, William, 72
Mayo, Lord, 28
Mehta, P.M., 83
Merriman, John Xavier, 5-6
Mesopotamia, 70, 93, 94
Meston, Sir James, 57, 58, 59, 73, 79, 91
Middle East, 110
Mill, James, 36
Mill, John Stuart, 76
Milner, Alfred, 7, 8-9, 18-19, 56

Minto, Lord, 29, 30, 56-7, 66, 76, 77
Moderates, 83, 84, 89, 122
Montagu, E.S., 31, 75, 80, 93, 94, 95, 98
Montagu-Chelmsford Report, 23, 30-1, 60, 87
Morgan, Ben H., 13
Morley, John, 29, 30, 52, 56, 66, 76, 77, 82, 83
Morley-Minto reforms, 29, 75, 77, 78, 82, 86, 88
Mountbatten, Lord, 116
Mountbattens, 117
Munro, Sir Thomas, 24
Muslim League. *See* All-India Muslim League
Mutiny. *See* Revolt of 1857

Naoroji, Dadabhai, 45, 76
Natal, 63
National Liberal Club, 11
Navigation Acts, 24
Nazism, 115
Nehru, Jawaharlal, 101, 103, 105, 106, 110-27
Newbolt, Henry, 12, 13
New Zealand, 7, 9, 34, 72
Non-co-operation movement, 99, 100
Northbrook, Lord, 64

Oliver, F.S., 10
Orange Free State, 29

Pakistan, 108, 117-18, 123
Pal, B.C., 3, 100
Paris, 74, 112
Parkin, G.R., 53
Parliament, 20, 22, 27, 29, 30, 38, 39, 40, 66, 67, 80, 103
Pennsylvania, 2
Persia, 70
Philips, C.H., 77
Pitt, William, 26, 27

Index

Pollock, Sir Frederick, 65
Portugal, 42
Portuguese empire, 33
Powell, E.T., 10
Problem of the Commonwealth, The, 15
Prussia, 13, 14, 31
Purna Swaraj. See Complete independence

'Quit India' movement, 115

Rao, Madhava, 46
Rau, B. N., 123
Restoration, 2
Revolt of 1857, 28, 35, 38, 39, 42, 43, 44, 106
Rhodes scholars, 56
Ripon, Lord, 28, 29
Roberts, Charles, 95
Rome, 15
Rosebery, Lord, 4-5
Round Table, 13, 57-61, 79, 82, 86, 87, 88
Round Table, 69, 81
Round Table Conference, 104, 107, 121
Rowlatt Act, 98
Royal Colonial Institute, 8, 10, 18, 51
Russia, 43, 46

Salisbury, Lord, 45, 53
Samuel, Lord, 121
Sardinia, 42
Sawtell, Arthur, 3
Second British Empire, 31, 96
Seeley, J.R., 5, 49
Seton, M.C., 86
Sevres, Treaty of, 98
Shafi, Sir Muhammad, 68
Shakespeare, William, 3
Shaw, Bernard, 5, 12
Shuckburgh, J. E., 86
Simla, 85

Simon Commission, 103
Sinha, Sir Satyendra Prasanna, 74, 84-5, 91
Smith, Goldwin, 5, 12, 24, 36, 37, 52, 76
Smith, Thomas, 3
Smuts, General, 15-16, 108-9
South Africa, 5, 19, 23, 30, 34, 72, 97, 102, 108, 109, 111, 121
South African War, 11, 97
Spain, 45
Spanish empire, 33
Standard of Empire, 8
Statute of Westminster, 105
Sterling area, 124
Strangways, H.B.T., 51
Studies in Mid-Victorian Imperialism, 33
Soviet Union, 116, 123
Swaraj, 80, 99, 100, 102, 111

Third British Empire, 31, 96
Thirteen Colonies, 20, 23, 26, 33, 35
Tilak, B.G., 92, 98, 100
Times, The, 11, 91
Times of India, 89-90
Tories. See Conservatives
Toronto, 61
Transvaal, 29
Turgot, 33
Turkey, 42, 98

United Nations, 108, 126
United States of America, 2, 4, 13, 21, 23, 35, 39, 43, 47, 116

Vendredi, 112
Victoria, Queen, 11, 20, 62
Virginia, 2
Virginia Company, 18

War Cabinet, 72, 83, 93, 94, 95
War Office, 55

Wedgwood, Josiah, 79
Wellesley, Lord, 36
Wellington, Duke of, 30
White, Arnold, 9-10
Williams, David, 2
Willingdon, Lord, 83, 92
Wilson, James, 3
World War, First, 13, 31, 60, 67, 68, 69, 70, 82, 83, 86, 97

World War, Second, 16, 105, 108

Young, Frederick, 50

Zimmern, A.E., 14, 15, 31, 32, 96
Zulu rebellion, 97